Bobby Rahal: The Graceful Champion

Bobby Rahal
The Graceful Champion

by Gordon Kirby

Foreword by Nigel Roebuck

Introduction by David Letterman

Design By Tom Morgan

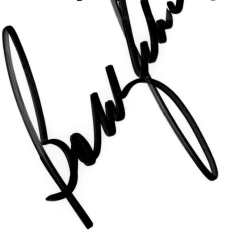

DAVID BULL PUBLISHING

We recognize that some words, model names, and designations
mentioned in this book are the property of the trademark
holder. We use them only for identification purposes.

Library of Congress Cataloging-in-Publication Data

Kirby, Gordon
    Bobby Rahal : the graceful champion /
    by Gordon Kirby : introduction by David
    Letterman ; foreword by Nigel Roebuck.
        p.   cm.
    Includes index.
    ISBN 0-9649722-8-X (hc.)
    1. Rahal, Bobby, 1953-   . 2. Automobile racing drivers—
United States Biography.   I. Title.
GV 1032.R35B63   1999
796.72'092—dc21
[B]
                        99-27309
                            CIP

David Bull Publishing, logo, and colophon are trademarks of
David Bull Publishing, Inc.

Book and cover design:
Tom Morgan, Blue Design, Portland, Maine
(www.bluedes.com)

Printed in Hong Kong

10 9 8 7 6 5 4 3 2 1

David Bull Publishing
4250 East Camelback Road
Suite K150
Phoenix, AZ 85018
602-852-9500
602-852-9503 (fax)

www.bullpublishing.com

Acknowledgments:

Without the enthusiasm and sharp recollections provided by
Bobby and Debi Rahal, and by Bobby's parents, Mike and Barb, this
book would not have been possible. Their involvement and love of
motorsports made presenting Bobby's story a pleasure.

A particular thanks to Bobby's personal secretary, Linda Lett,
who makes order of Bobby's busy life, and helped coordinate many
elements of the book. Other members of Team Rahal made similar
contributions, including Scott Reisz, Julie Klausner, Tom Blattler,
Scott Roembke, and Larry "Ramjet" Randlett. Thanks also to Tim
Cindric, Jim Prescott, and all the technical minds and hands at
Team Rahal for allowing me to work among them from time to
time.

Bobby's former teammates, competitors, and business associates
have been both generous with their time and candid in their inter-
views. I am grateful to Bob Garretson, Barry Green, Steve and
Christine Horne, Carl Hogan, Adrian Newey, Brian Redman,
Adrian Reynard, Keke Rosberg, Doug Shierson, Al Unser Jr., and
Franz Weis for their considerable help in providing information,
and to Honda's Nobuhiko Kawamoto, Tom Elliott, Michihiro
Asaka, and Robert Clarke.

A special thanks to Bobby's partner David Letterman, my col-
league Nigel Roebuck, Ferrari S.p.A.'s Moira Martin and Riccardo
Andreoni, my transcriber Donna Seavey, and Steve Spence for giving the manuscript a thoughtful read.

Finally, I would like to thank old friend and associate Paul
Webb for gathering and editing this huge selection of photographs
from Bobby's career, plus an outstanding group of photographers,
including Dan Boyd, Michael C. Brown, Rich Chenet, Hal
Crocker, Jon Eisberg, Art Flores, Gary Gold, Bob Harmeyer,
Geoff Hewitt, Lee Self, Marc Sproule, Steve Swope, Bob
Tronolone, and LAT Photographic. Their work has brought this
book vividly to life. —*G.K.*

Page 1: Crew chief Jimmy Prescott guides Bobby into his pit stall during practice at the California Speedway in 1998. The Fontana event was Bobby's last race as a driver. (Paul Webb)

Page 2: Bobby rests on the Armco barrier along the pit lane during practice at the Nazarath Speedway in 1997. (Michael C. Brown).

Right: "John Trueman was Mike's mechanic on the Carrera 6 in 1970," Bobby says. "I'm seventeen, and we're at a race at Watkins Glen." (Rahal collection)

Pages 4-5: In his last appearance at Long Beach, Bobby qualified on the outside of the front row, led the race, and turned the fastest lap, but his chance at winning was thwarted by an early multicar incident that left him stalled and stranded for five laps. (Paul Webb)

Page 8: Winning the trophy was gratifying, but it meant little compared to Bobby's huge satisfaction after fending off a late challenge from Mario Andretti at the Meadowlands in 1987. (Dan Boyd)

Introduction
David Letterman

Bobby Rahal is a champion who made winning look easy and graceful. All of us have our favorite Bobby Rahal memory—his Indy 500 victory in 1986, his third Champ car title in 1992, his whirlwind courtship of Cher, and so many more.

It's no secret that I have a great fondness and respect for Bobby. What you may not know is how often I put on my Team Rahal suit and race around the office in a swivel chair. Don't kid yourself, it's very close to the real thing.

As we all know, motorsports is a metaphor for life: great success only comes from fanatical attention to detail, split-second timing, and the perfect coordination of movement and music. Or is that synchronized swimming?

But to you the reader, let me say something Bobby might be too embarrassed to mention: *Don't steal this book*. A lot of hard work went into the writing, printing, binding, and shipping; believe me—it adds up, Chief. We *all* get a cut. Many bookstores have state-of-the-art theft-detection systems, and they *do* prosecute shoplifters.

Enjoy the book, and keep the shiny side up...whatever the hell that means.

DAVE LETTERMAN
Team Rahal Co-Owner/America's Most Beloved TV Personality

Above: David Letterman enjoys himself at the races, away from the daily pressures of producing his very successful, New York City–based *Late Night* television show. (Dan Boyd)

Opposite: After the 1998 Marlboro 500 at the California Speedway, David Letterman joins Bobby in victory circle to congratulate the top three finishers: Jimmy Vasser, Greg Moore, and Alex Zanardi (not in the photo). The November 1 event was Bobby's last race as a driver. (Paul Webb)

Foreword
Nigel Roebuck

Through the years I have seen Bobby Rahal race many cars in many places, but at the mention of his name I think instinctively not of Indianapolis or Milwaukee, Brands Hatch or Monte Carlo, but of a rather more parochial setting: the Barley Mow, my local pub in West Horsley, Surrey.

An unusual place, this. At a glance it is an archetypal English country pub, complete with beams and the like, but on the walls you find not hunting or fishing scenes, but paintings of Tazio Nuvolari or Jimmy Clark, together with photographs—taken outside the front door—of racing folk from Stirling Moss to Al Unser Jr.

When Bobby walked in there, his eye was soon caught by a Michael Turner print. "Ha! A Lotus 47. Jeez, my dad had one of those when I was just starting, in '73. Awful thing! The next car I drove was a Lola, and it mystified me because its steering wheel didn't shake all over the place. I'd thought that's what all race cars did...."

He was in his element. "After you've lived here for a while, as I did in the '70s," he said, "forever after you always miss English pubs. I love an atmosphere like this." Drink? "A pint of bitter, please—what else?"

Above: Lunch at the Barley Mow in December 1997. Seated at the table are (counterclockwise) author Gordon Kirby; Bobby; English motorsports writers Nigel Roebuck, Eoin Young, and Maurice Hamilton; and the Newman-Haas team's John Szymanski. Just visible at left is Bobby's wife, Debi. (Gary Gold)

Opposite: At the Goodwood Festival of Speed in 1998, Bobby prepares to drive an ex–Roger McCluskey 1968 Eagle-Offenhauser turbo. This was the first time he drove a car powered by the legendary "Offy" engine. Beside him is a Lotus 25 F1 car from 1963. (Paul Webb)

To this day, the one major regret of Rahal's professional life is that he never competed regularly in Formula One; indeed, touched it only briefly, and then quite early in his career. The lamented Gilles Villeneuve, looking back on his years in Formula Atlantic, told me once that "Keke [Rosberg] and Bobby were the only guys I ever worried about," iron-clad proof in itself that Rahal had the talent to make it in Formula One, should the right opportunity arise.

That particular card never fell for him, however, and it may not have been his complete loss, for, as one who has been writing about it for more than twenty-five years, I have to wonder if so civilized a man could easily have coped with so precious and insular an environment.

Bobby is such a well-rounded individual, that's the point. Unlike most drivers, for one thing, he has a deep knowledge of motor racing history, and cares deeply for the heritage of the sport to which he has devoted his life. It was typical of him that, on a weekend off between the Detroit and Portland Champ car races in 1998, he accepted an offer to take part in the Goodwood Festival of Speed. Typical, too, that he raved like a schoolboy about the cars he saw there.

Ultimately, though, what makes Rahal such great company is that he is aware of the wider world, able to talk about all manner of subjects, and with authority and wit. This is unusual, to say the least, in one of his profession.

In the course of a long career, Bobby raced virtually every type of car, but history will remember him as the winner of the Indianapolis 500 in 1986. Although one thinks of him first as a road racer, some of his greatest drives were on ovals, and no one, in my experience, has ever better conveyed how it is to be strapped into something skimming along the walls at close to 4 miles a minute.

"Self-preservation," he once said to me, laconic as usual, "was always very high on my agenda. And one thing I learned quickly was that, on an oval, you cannot drive around a handling problem—or not for long, anyway. To me, the late stages of a 500-miler were the most dangerous time, because you'd be running at 220 or so, and there'd be guys dragging around at 180. Big differential.

Bobby runs flat out in 1986 at Indianapolis, the site of his greatest individual victory. Bobby began his career as a road racer but quickly mastered the techniques of oval racing. He scored ten of his twenty-four Champ car victories on ovals. (Rich Chenet)

"You could have bad moments like that, and when you complained to a guy afterwards, he'd say, 'Well, if your car was handling like mine, you'd be slow.' I'd say, 'Look, if my car was handling like yours, I'd park it.'"

When Rahal was really on it, the car working as it should, he was truly formidable. Clashing schedules have always kept me from attending more than the odd Champ car race, but I was there at Phoenix in 1992 for Bobby's first event as a team owner as well as a driver. He comfortably took the pole, then proceeded to lead every one of the 200 laps in as dominant a drive as I have ever seen.

When it came time for "Rahal's Last Ride" in 1998, I hoped he would win a race in his final season, and there were times, notably at Long Beach, when it seemed he might, but in the end I was pleased simply to see him walk away from it. Racing may be immeasurably less perilous than it was, but however much one might lament the retirement of a driver of his stature, still there are always minglings of relief. How many hearts skipped how many beats when that white car—on its side—came skittering down the road at Motegi?

I feel honoured, as a Brit, to have been asked to write the foreword for Gordon Kirby's biography of this great American racing driver, whose achievements I have savoured, whose friendship I have enjoyed for many years. Read on and you will understand why.

Bobby started his third championship season in 1992 by dominating the 200-mile race at Phoenix International Raceway, leading every lap. Here he pulls away from Emerson Fittipaldi, Mario Andretti, Paul Tracy, and Rick Mears. (Rich Chenet)

"Here I am doing what I do best—cleaning!" Bobby says. Mike drove the Alfa Romeo in the Meadowdale Raceway Inaugural in 1958. "Those were the days when sports cars were driven to the circuit with the family packed in, and then raced." Mike says. (Rahal collection)

"It was a nutrient-rich environment."

As he pressed the throttle pedal and powered his Elva-Porsche Mk VII through the Carousel turn and accelerated along the tree-shaded stretch toward Canada Corner, engine howling, the wind tugging at his helmet and goggles, Mike Rahal was as happy as any man could be. It was a fine July afternoon in 1967, and he and his co-driver, Ralph Trieschmann, were running a close second in the under 2-liter class at Mike's favorite racetrack, Road America. Horst Kwech was in the lead driving a sleek Porsche 904 in the annual 500-mile Sports Car Club of America (SCCA) classic.

Mike's silver Elva-Porsche was the car in which his oldest son, Bobby, would make his racing debut three years later, but that summer afternoon the fourteen-year-old Bobby was in the pits, calling the shots on his dad's pit strategy.

"Bobby was involved in a big way by then," Mike recalls. "He knew it was very critical late in the race whether you stopped for fuel. Everybody was running very tight on fuel, so Bobby showed a sign saying 'Fuel,' but he only showed it to Horst Kwech, and Kwech thought we were running out of fuel, so he decided he could stop for fuel. He came 'round and went into the pits, and I was right behind him, and I kept going, and we won!"

Mike's enthusiasm for cars and racing was utterly infectious, and Bobby already was demonstrating the studied wiliness that would serve him so well in the years ahead. Bobby's first race at seventeen was a telling preview of what would develop, through a series of

Above: Mike Rahal (wearing the helmet) confers with co-driver Werner Frank during a race weekend at Watkins Glen in 1970. The two also co-drove at Sebring in 1970 and 1971. Bobby and Dick Jacobs are in the background. (Rahal collection)

difficult shifts in his career path and personal life, into one of America's most successful and respected racing careers.

It all started in the garage beside Mike Rahal's red brick house in Glen Ellyn, Illinois, a leafy, wooded western suburb of Chicago. A self-made fruit and food wholesaler and distributor, Mike was able as his business grew to indulge himself on weekends in his passion for motor racing. He kept a succession of sports and racing cars in the garage beside the house at 934 Crescent Boulevard that he and his wife Barbara moved into in 1962, when Bobby was nine.

Mike raced for the first time in 1957, aboard an Austin-Healey 100 Le Mans, on an infield road course at the Wisconsin State Fair Park, now known as the Milwaukee Mile. An SCCA member, Mike raced at all the nearby upper Midwest road circuits, such as Meadowdale and Blackhawk Farms in Illinois; Grattan, Michigan; and, of course, a family favorite, Road America in Elkhart Lake, Wisconsin.

He owned a series of production sports cars, as well as real sports racers, including a rear-engine Cooper-Climax, an Elva-Climax and Elva-Porsche, a Porsche Carrera 6, and a Lotus 47. Mike and a handful of his friends and mechanics maintained the cars. In the intoxicating atmosphere of that playground, off to the side of the Rahals' home, Bobby was introduced to the sport.

"When I was in grade school, the summers to me were Little League and racing," Bobby fondly recalls. "But as I grew older, baseball was out, and it became more and more racing. I grew up at places like Elkhart Lake, and around cars in general. There were always race cars around our house. It was a very heady environment to grow up in.

"My father raced as a hobby, and in terms of family priorities, it was probably about tenth. For us it was fun. We all got involved in it, but there was never any thought of my being a professional driver. It was assumed I would go through high school and then college, and then I would have a career. If you wanted to race, well, you know, you would be a weekend warrior."

The Rahal family came from an area in Syria that is now Lebanon. Mike's father, George, emigrated to the United States in 1911, settling in Rhode Island and working in the shipyards of Fall River, Massachusetts, immediately after World War I. George Rahal went back to his homeland in 1919 to marry his wife, Louise, before returning to the United States for good in 1920. He moved to Cleveland, Ohio, and began to carve out a living selling and trading textiles door-to-door. His third son, Mike,

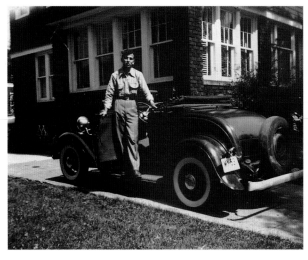

was born in 1924, and Mike and older brother, David, grew up in Ohio amid sprightly family conversation and an abiding spirit of entrepreneurship.

"It was always the ambition of anybody with Semitic blood to get off and be an entrepreneur of some kind," Mike remarks about his father and family. "It was almost an article of faith that the Arab business people first sold linens and rags from house to house and progressed from there to the next level of enterprise."

Mike's uncle also moved to Cleveland, and through hard work and self-reliance, the Rahal families survived the Depression. Mike explains: "In our culture, the Arab culture, to accept relief, or the dole, was totally unacceptable. We were all expected to pull our own weight." Not long after the United States was drawn into World War II following the bombing of Pearl Harbor in 1941 by the Japanese, Mike, eighteen, joined the Navy. He went to war as a torpedoman aboard the destroyer *USS MacDonough* and was in eighteen major engagements in the Pacific, which involved, among other actions, sinking two Japanese submarines and intercepting three Japanese kamikaze aircraft. Mike was discharged from the Navy in January 1946, and almost by chance found himself as a student at Denison College in Granville, Ohio, then roughly a three-hour drive south of Cleveland.

The brother of a friend of Mike's from high school had graduated from Denison, and Mike was invited to join him on a trip to the college to take an entrance exam. During the war, Mike had taken some correspondence courses from the University of Wisconsin, and he passed the examination.

"I had a little bit of a head start, and the irony of it was I passed and my friend flunked the entrance exam," Mike says. "I stayed and had four of the most fabulous years of my life living in a small, encapsulated academic community with not more than 1,300 students, of which 400 were entering GIs. It was founded by the Baptists and was a school that had some strict ideas about discipline.

"They assumed that everyone who came there was culturally illiterate, and they weren't very far from the truth. And secondly, in order to be a college graduate one had to be versed in the king's English in writing, speech—every aspect. We went through vigorous examinations in which we had to write themes about interesting subjects, and when you wrote this theme, if it was assessed as an A, if you misspelled a word, it was a B. Two misspelled words and it was a C. Three wrong, you got a D. And the fourth, you got an F. You were to be a well-rounded individual with the ability to think, and basically, this had a very important effect on myself, and later on Bobby."

While he was at Denison, Mike got married, after a whirlwind courtship, to Barbara Woodward. "She was a bit forward," Mike remembers, smiling. "I was going into my junior year, and when we met, she blatantly invited me to dance. It didn't take long before I was determined to marry her. She had to obtain the permission of her parents because she wasn't twenty-one, and we lived on campus for two years."

After graduating, Mike (right) was a salesman for his uncle's business, Sunshine Packing, which processed and sold fruit juices. This was one of the first sales conventions Mike worked in 1950. A fellow salesman is on the left. The other man is unidentified. (Rahal collection)

After graduating from Denison in 1950, Mike went to work in Cleveland as a salesman for his uncle's business, Sunshine Packing, which processed and sold fruit juices. Drawing its raw materials from the fruit belt east of Cleveland through Erie, Pennsylvania, and into western New York state, the company had offices in New York and Chicago. Mike was on the road a lot, criss-crossing the Midwest and Northeast, selling. Eventually he decided to go out on his own, so he settled in Chicago and went into competition with his uncle and his brother David.

"It was the booming years of the frozen food industry," Mike says. "We came in and the horizons were unlimited. Then Bobby came along, and he was a wonderful boy. I had all kinds of dreams for him, all of which have been far exceeded."

Robert Woodward Rahal was born on January 10, 1953, when Mike and Barbara were

still living in Medina, Ohio, a suburb of Cleveland. Bobby was joined by a brother, Ian, five years later, by which time the family had moved to Glen Ellyn. Mike's two sons grew up in a house alive with talk of commerce, politics, history, reading, and motor racing.

Mike's interest in sports cars and motor racing began when he was at Denison. He remembers "hungering after" an MG TC on sale for $1,400 at a nearby dealership but being unable to afford the car.

"My red Triumph TR2 was one of the first brought into the U.S.," Mike says. "We never raced that car. It was a wicked car to handle. We're in front of the little house in Glen Ellyn, Illinois, where we first lived." (Rahal collection)

Later, when Mike was working for his uncle in Cleveland, the young Rahal couple bought a Triumph TR2, and it was this car that gave toddler Bobby his first taste of sporting motoring. "It was red, sleek, the culmination of the fire in your belly," Mike remembers. "I saw it and went into the lot, and in twenty minutes I owned it. The TR2 had to be put together by some diabolical being. It certainly didn't drive well, and it rode like a buckboard, but that car looked good. It had louvers all over it. We sputtered around in that. Bobby used to love to ride in the passenger seat."

Mike's first exposure to racing happened after he struck out on his own and moved his family to Chicago. While living in Chicago, a neighbor suggested they go up to Elkhart Lake, to watch SCCA sports car races through the streets of that rural vacation hamlet. For Mike and his oldest son, it was a fateful trip.

"I came home, and my blood was up," Mike says. "We sold the TR2 and bought an Austin-Healey 100 Le Mans with straps and louvers all over it. It was really something. So we went to Milwaukee for my first race, and I won! The favorite was a fellow who sort of threw his keys out on the grid as if he was in a class of his own, and everybody ran for second place. Well, I beat him. He had a similar Healey, so I thought, Boy, this is duck soup! What's so hard about this?"

Barbara jumps in, laughing at the memory. "It's dangerous to win your first race." Indeed, the harsh realities of racing were driven home very clearly in Mike's second race, on the brand-new, purpose-built 4-mile Road America road course just south of the old Elkhart Lake street circuit.

"There were several D-type Jaguars and Coopers there, and I was badly outclassed," Mike says. "Well, I was trying to pass Walt Hansgen at turn eleven, and I got on the wrong side. I was on the right side, and you should be on the left side as you go through there, and the front end washed out, and I went about a third of the way down the straight and finally ended up against a tree."

Mike broke his leg badly and was speared by the steering wheel. "I got out and waved to the crowd to show my bravado, and I lost everything. I collapsed." He was in the hospital for sixteen days.

"They had to redo my knee, and my ribs were cracked, and many of my fillings came out, I hit with such force. They put me in an ambulance, and all I can remember is that the ambulance driver had been nursing a whiskey bottle. It took me about four months to recover, and then there ensued a huge amount of guilt. Here I was, a young married man with two kids and a third on the way, and how irresponsible it was."

Before starting his first day of kindergarten in 1958, Bobby poses against Mike's Alfa Romeo Sprint Veloce. (Rahal collection)

Bobby, Mike, Ian, and two boys from next door, Po and Ted, make the starting lineup for a touch football game in Glen Ellyn, Illinois, in 1961. (Rahal collection)

The accident sidelined Mike from racing for a while, although he was soon out shopping for something to replace his crashed Healey. He went through a series of cars before he settled on a 1,300cc Alfa Romeo Sprint Veloce coupe.

"The Alfa wasn't very competitive. It was heavy, with a steel body. Meanwhile, Bobby was developing a sophistication in racing. He was getting to know all the cars, who was who. Reminds me of his son Graham today."

Mike decided that racing mere production cars was no longer for him, so he bought his first real sports racer, an 1,100 Coventry Climax–powered, rear-engine Cooper. From that car he traded up to a quicker Elva Mk VI with a similar Climax engine and then to a newer Elva Mk VII, powered by another four-cylinder Climax engine. The next move was to install a 2-liter Porsche Spyder engine in the Mk VII Elva with the help of north Chicago Porsche dealer Ollie Schmidt. With that car in 1967 Mike won the under-2-liter class in the 500-mile United States Road Racing Championship round at Elkhart Lake, beating Horst Kwech, thanks to Bobby's keen pit-side gamesmanship.

The Elva-Porsche introduced the Rahal family to Hartmut Leuschner, who was one of Ollie Schmidt's Porsche racing mechanics. "He could do anything," Mike says. "He could rebuild a chassis, anything. Bobby used to be his shadow. He learned a lot from Hartmut."

The teenage Bobby was also honing his skills as a salesman and middleman, successfully urging his father to sell the Elva and buy an all-enclosed Porsche 906 (known simply as a Carrera 6). "Bobby got on my back something fierce," Mike grimaces. "I don't even know

Barb, Ian, and Bobby take a harbor tour to Fort Sumter in Charleston, South Carolina, in 1959. This was a stop on their return trip from Fort Myers, Florida, where they had driven in Mike's Alfa Giulietta, raced the car, vacationed, then drove back to Ohio. (Rahal collection)

"This is me at Elkhart," Bobby admits. "I must be with the greasy-haired kids—Bill Banger and those guys—because Bill always wore that hat. I don't know how I ended up wearing it on that occasion." (Rahal collection)

how I said yes, but the next thing I know he's in a phone booth next to the concession stand calling the guy that owned this 906, and the next thing I knew, I bought it."

Another important influence on Bobby's life during this time was Bill Banger, a friend who was a few years older than Bobby. "He and his buddies were really into cars, and they used to come down to our house," Bobby reminisces. "In those days, everybody was into surfing and cars, the Beach Boys, Jan & Dean, and all that kind of good stuff. I was ten years old, and he was like a big brother. He set the style."

Banger now runs a car dealership in Coeur d'Alene, Idaho. He took Bobby to all the local racing venues like Santa Fe Speedway to see stock car and motorcycle races, and to O'Hare airport in Chicago, where there used to be a quarter-mile paved oval, and to the drag races at the U.S. 30 dragstrip.

"One of Billy's buddies had a 426 Dodge Hemi. Another guy had a Porsche, and, of course, at home Mike had his cars. It was such an unbelievable environment for me as a ten-year-old kid because I was around cars all the time, and all we did was talk about cars and motorcycles.

"It was a very traumatic time for me when he was drafted and got sent to Fort Ord for a couple of years of duty, which was good for him because he was next door to Laguna Seca. But I thought he was going away forever, and I was just a mess. I was so disappointed."

"Bobby used to go out in that kart and beat anybody else's time," Mike says. The kart belonged to Bobby's cousin, Hal, who drove it around the backyard of his family's house in Medina. The photo was taken in 1964, around the time that Bobby started wearing glasses. (Rahal collection)

It was in these surroundings that Bobby grew up, moving steadily, almost inexorably, into a career in racing. "I had such an undying love for automobiles and the sport. It came from my father's interests, and I really grabbed hold of it," he says. "Some of the experiences over the years were just hilarious. I can remember trailer hitches breaking, trailers detaching from the car, and half-assed fixes for serious problems. We jerry-rigged things. You think back and say, 'My God!' But in those days, everybody went racing that way to a certain degree."

Bobby remembers going with Mike to buy gearbox parts from current Champ car team owner Carl Haas when Haas was working out of his mother's basement. Among other businesses, the Chicago-based Haas has owned and operated Newman-Haas Racing, the second most successful Championship Auto Racing Teams (CART) contender, since 1983, and has been a successful team owner, with both CanAm and Formula 5000 cars, for more than thirty years.

"People see Carl Haas today, and I tell them I remember going to his mother's basement, and they have a hard time believing me. But for me, loving cars, it was like a nutrient-rich environment to grow up in. All the things that happened, and all the people I got to know over the years—it was very, very special."

"When we first got the Porsche Carrera 6, which was in late '68," Bobby says, "we took it up and down Crescent Boulevard, just for kicks. That's Mike at the wheel and that's our Porsche 911 parked there. He says I suckered him into buying this car." (Rahal collection)

"It just electrified me."

At the wheel of the Carrera 6, Mike won the SCCA's Chicago region B/Sports-racing title in 1968. He went to the club's national championship runoffs, which took place that year at Riverside, California, but as Bobby says, "we got our butts kicked." For three years, however, starting in 1969, Mike, with sixteen-year-old Bobby as strategist and crew chief, took part in two races that were very important to them—Florida's Sebring 12 Hours and New York's Watkins Glen 6 Hours. Mike co-drove his Carrera 6 at Sebring in 1969 with Bill Stroh, and again with Werner Frank and Hugh Wise in 1970 and 1971. Stroh had a Ph.D. in chemistry and worked for a local Chicago company. Frank ran a Toyota dealership in South Elgin, Illinois, and drove in SCCA and the International Motor Sports Association (IMSA) races. Wise was a chemist who lived nearby in Downer's Grove and whose father played for the Chicago White Sox.

"Our great moment was when we went to Sebring," Mike proudly recalls. "Talk about being unprepared or unsophisticated, running against the factory teams. We were pitted right next to the Alfa Romeo factory team. In '69, my co-driver crashed the car, but in 1970, we won. Rico Steineman [Porsche's factory team manager] came down the pits late at night

Above: In 1969 Mike (shown in the car) debuted his Carrera 6 at Sebring with co-drivers Bill Stroh and Hugh Wise. They did not finish the race because damage from a crash during Wise's stint forced their retirement. (Ken Breslauer collection)

Opposite: Mike helps Hugh Wise climb into the car during a night pit stop and driver change at Sebring in 1970. Driving the Porsche Carrera 6, they won their class and beat the factory teams of Porsche, Alfa Romeo, and Ferrari. Ed Sexton cleans the windshield. (Hal Crocker)

about the tenth or eleventh hour to take a look at us and say 'Hello, you're leading your class.' Bobby was so elated.

"Behind us was Alfa Romeo, Ferrari, and the Porsche team. We did really well that year. Bobby ran the sign board, and we had a two-way radio setup, but that went west in the first twenty minutes because we were on the same frequency as the helicopter!

"That was my biggest win, without question," Mike adds. "We started the race with seventy-five cars and about forty finished. We were running behind [Jacky] Ickx and [Mario] Andretti and [Steve] McQueen. We also won the team trophy with another 906 driven by Doc Rosen."

By this time Bobby was seventeen and raring to drive. "He used to drive the cars around in the pits," Mike remembers. "Les Greibling, who owned Mid-Ohio, came over to me once and said, 'Rahal, if I see that kid of yours in your car again, you're out!' In later years we said, 'Well, Les, now what do you think?' Bobby got into the swing of it. He read every book, every magazine. He knew everything there was to know about racing."

Bobby's memories of those races at Sebring come rolling back. "I think those may have been the greatest races Sebring had with the factory Alfas, Matras, Ferraris, and Porsches, and you had the greatest drivers in the world there," Bobby enthuses. "The Matras had [François] Cevert and [Dan] Gurney in one car. And you had [Henri] Pescarolo and Johnny Servoz-Gavin in the other one. Then there were the factory Alfas, which had guys like [Rolf]

Above: Nanni Galli steers his Alfa Romeo Tipo 33-3 into a turn. The 1969 event was a disaster for the Alfa team. All three factory-entered cars dropped out in the first hour. During his career, Galli also drove for the Ferrari world sports car championship team and occasionally raced Formula One. (Ken Breslauer collection)

Right: "This is the way racing should be!" Bobby says of the Sebring 12 Hours' golden age. In the foreground at the start of the 1969 race are the factory Porsche 908s of Brian Redman and Jo Siffert (31) and Gerhard Mitter and Udo Schutz (29); the Ferrari 312P of Chris Amon and Mario Andretti (25); and the Lola Chevrolet driven by Mark Donohue and Ronnie Bucknam (9). (Ken Breslauer collection)

Stommelen and Nanni Galli, [Nino] Vacarella, Helmut Marko, and Ronnie Peterson. Porsche had [Vic] Elford, [Ricardo] Rodriguez, [Joe] Siffert, [Brian] Redman, the whole nine yards. It was awesome. Ferrari had Andretti and [Clay] Regazzoni. It was so neat in those days because all the Formula One drivers raced sports cars as well.

"The years my dad raced at Sebring and the Glen were filled with such unbelievably great racing. At the Glen, they'd run the 6 Hours on Saturday and a bunch of those guys would run their sports cars—Porsche 917s and Ferrari 512s—in the CanAm race on Sunday. I loved that. If there was an era I wished I could have driven in it would have been that era, the late '60s, early '70s."

For all the pressure that such a time-consuming avocation can place on a household, Bobby says he doesn't remember a single cross word about racing between his mom and dad. "My father wasn't one of these guys who took your college fund and went out and bought a race car with it," Bobby makes the point. "I think my mother must have had a lot of faith in me, because I never remember her saying, 'I wish you wouldn't do this. I wish you'd do something else.' "

Above: At Sebring in 1971, Bobby peers down the pit lane at night while Tom Peacock works on the Carrera 6's engine. "The thing had run like a freight train all day," Bobby says. But in the last hour, as they ran seventh overall, an oil line broke and took the car out of the race. (Rahal collection)

In 1970, Mike took his family on a European vacation that included visits to the Lola and Chevron race-car building shops, as well as the Monaco GP. "He would go to Europe every year to do business, and he would take my brother and me, ostensibly to teach us and give us some culture," Bobby explains. "Of course, I was seventeen, my girlfriend was back in Chicago, and all I wanted to do was do the racing car stuff and go home. I didn't want to deal with Windsor Castle and all that kind of stuff.

"We went to Lola, where they were building the T210 sports car, a beautiful little car. Then we went up to northern England and went to Chevron. They were building the B16 coupe, and everything in those days was so primitive. At Chevron, they built the cars on dirt floors.

"I think maybe to entertain us or shut us up my dad said, 'Well, let's go to see Monaco'. We went down to the race, and we're walking down the streets and we hear some cars coming down the hill behind us. In those days, they used to keep the cars at various garages around town and drive them down to the pits for practice. And here came the BRMs, which was Rodriguez and Siffert, and the noise just shattering off the buildings was fantastic.

"One of the things I'll give my father a lot of credit for is his ability to figure out a way. We had no tickets, so we get there and start wandering around. The day before, we wandered up and got into the grandstands at the hairpin for the Formula Three race. Nobody cared about the F3 race, so there was nobody there, and we said to the ticket guy, 'Remember us, we're coming back tomorrow.' So my father bribes the guy, and the next day for the F1 race the grandstand is packed at 120 percent of its capacity. I mean, don't

During their European trip the Rahal family visited the Provence region of France. Barb gives the boys an impromptu art history lesson as she points out aspects of the deteriorating mural on the side of the building. (Rahal collection)

Bobby took this photo at the Monaco Grand Prix in 1970, just after Jack Brabham slid into the haybales in front of where the Rahals were sitting. Brabham's mistake cost him the race but, he managed to salvage second place behind winner Jochen Rindt. (Rahal collection)

In his first race at Harewood Acres in southwestern Ontario, Canada, Bobby immediately showed his ability. "The Elva-Porsche was a great car," Mike says. "Ollie Schmidt had three of them, and they were very competitive in the United States Road Racing Championship. It had a state-of-the-art, four-cam Spyder motor." (Rahal collection)

There were two novice races held that day at Harewood, which had originally been an airfield. In the first, Bobby took the lead on the opening lap, then lapped the entire field before he spun on the rain-slicked surface. Mike says he slid about a quarter of a mile off the course. (Rahal collection)

get up and go to the bathroom, because somebody will be right there to take your seat. But the guy had seats for us there.

"This was the year when [Jack] Brabham crashed on the last lap and [Jochen] Rindt won. With about twenty laps to go, my parents said, 'Let's leave.' I said, 'No, no.' Rindt was catching him, and sure enough he started reeling Brabham in, lap after lap. I've got a picture from down in the grandstands, and you can see a television camera and cameraman, and right in front of him, just to the side, is Brabham with the nose of the car stuffed into the hay bales, and there's Rindt in the background of the picture."

"It was exciting, and we just had a great time. My brother and I basically made my parents miserable the rest of the trip because we'd seen what we wanted to see. We wanted to go home, and they had to do the things they really came for."

For Bobby, there was one more memory from that weekend that stayed with him. "I remember in Nice a guy in a Lamborghini Miura came by, and it almost seemed like it had an unmuffled, straight exhaust. It just electrified me. I said, 'This is what it's all about.' We didn't have that in the States. What I saw that weekend was everything I thought it was going to be and more. That's why racing in Europe for me was never something I thought I *had* to do. It was something I wanted to do."

The time had come for Bobby to drive his first race. He was only seventeen in 1970, old enough to race in Canada but not the United States, where the SCCA's minimum age was twenty-one. So Mike and Bobby drove across the border into Ontario to a Canadian race-track, Harewood Acres, an airport circuit located south of the small city of London, close to Lake Erie. In his first race, on May 21, 1970, Bobby drove the Elva-Porsche that his dad had sold to Hugh Wise.

"My dad was racing the Elva," Bobby recalls, "and I drove it in a novice race in which anybody with anything could run, from Mini-Coopers to formula cars. I'd love to know where that Elva-Porsche is now. It's worth about $400,000, and I think my dad sold it to Hugh Wise for $3,500 and hurriedly cashed the check before Hugh changed his mind!"

There were two novice races at Harewood that May day. Driving one of the faster cars among a wide selection of racing machinery, Bobby stormed into the lead on the opening lap and ran away, lapping the field before he spun off. Later in the afternoon he started the second novice race dead last in a field of thirty-seven and finished a steadier eleventh, turning the race's fastest lap.

"He did real well," Mike remembers with pride. "He was leading by over a lap, and it had rained and the water

Bobby and Mike at Indianapolis Raceway Park in 1970. "While Mike was in Europe on business, we had stripped the Carrera 6, got rid of all the Bondo, and repainted it," Bobby says. "He crashed it the first lap of the race. He diced with Doug Shierson before some Corvettes spun at the first turn and a guy T-boned him." (Rahal collection)

Racing History

1. Harewood Acres, Ontario, May 21, 1970. Type of car: Elva-Porsche 1800c.c. Race #1- Started eighth out of twenty-one cars. Lapped entire field in six laps, won by 1 lap, 32 seconds. Race #2- Started thirty-seventh out of thirty-seven cars. Race was ten laps in length. Finished 11th overall and set new lap record for novices at 1 min. 17 sec.

2. Harewood Acres, Ontario, Canada. Type of car: Elva-Porsche 1800. Race #1- Finished third out of eighteen cars. Race #2- Was running second when cooling fan broke resulting in a DNF. August 4, 1970.

3. Mosport Park, Ontario, Canada. Type of car: Porsche Carrera 6. June 21, 1971. Race #1- Started on pole position and won by 31 sec. Race #2- Started on pole position. Battled with Group 7 car for 14 laps, spun and finished second. Set new lap record for novices at 2 min, 32 sec. Avg. 98.7 m. p.h.

4. Watkins Glen, N.Y. Type of car: Lotus 47 1600 c.c. IMSA Three Hours of Endurance. Back of the grid due to mechanical problems. Finished 16th after running 11th for two and a half hours. Fell back due to loss of oil pressure. Co-drove with Michael Rahal and Horst Kroll.

Robert W. Rahal
March 22, 1973

In the second novice race, Bobby started last in a field of thirty-seven and finished eleventh. He also turned the race's fastest lap. (Rahal collection)

Opposite: Bobby's own account of his early races, written in 1973. He believed he had won his first race, forgeting he had actually spun off after blitzing the field. Talking to him now, he also insists he raced only once at Harewood, and Mike agrees.

didn't drain very well. Bobby drove the car in too deep and got about a quarter of a mile down the runway, off the course. I raced that weekend as well. We just cleaned the car up and ran it in a few races for both of us. We didn't do any service to the car. We didn't know any better."

A few months later Bobby again raced the Elva-Porsche at Harewood in a pair of novice races. He took third in the first race and was running second in the other race when a cooling fan broke, bringing him into the pits. The following year Bobby started in two more Canadian novice races, this time at Mosport, a fast, challenging road course northeast of Toronto that hosted the Canadian Grand Prix almost every year from 1967 to 1977. At Mosport in June of 1971, Bobby drove the Porsche Carrera 6 that Mike had raced successfully at Sebring and elsewhere. He started both races from the pole, winning by half a minute the first time out and finishing second after spinning in the second race.

"He was barely eighteen and boy," Mike glows at the memory. "He ran away with his novice race there. He drove beautifully. I didn't drive that day at all. I thought I'd lost my seat forever." For his part, Bobby wasn't at all sure that he was cut out for the racing business. "It scared the living daylights out of me. I thought, 'No way. This isn't for me.' "

Later in the year, Mike sold the 906 and Bobby went off to college at Denison. For more than a year, Mike was without a racing car, and the Rahal family went missing from the SCCA's Midwestern racing scene for the first time in almost fifteen years. It seemed like the time had come for Bobby to forget about racing and get on with his education and life. Says Bobby, "It was the end of this era of us all being together."

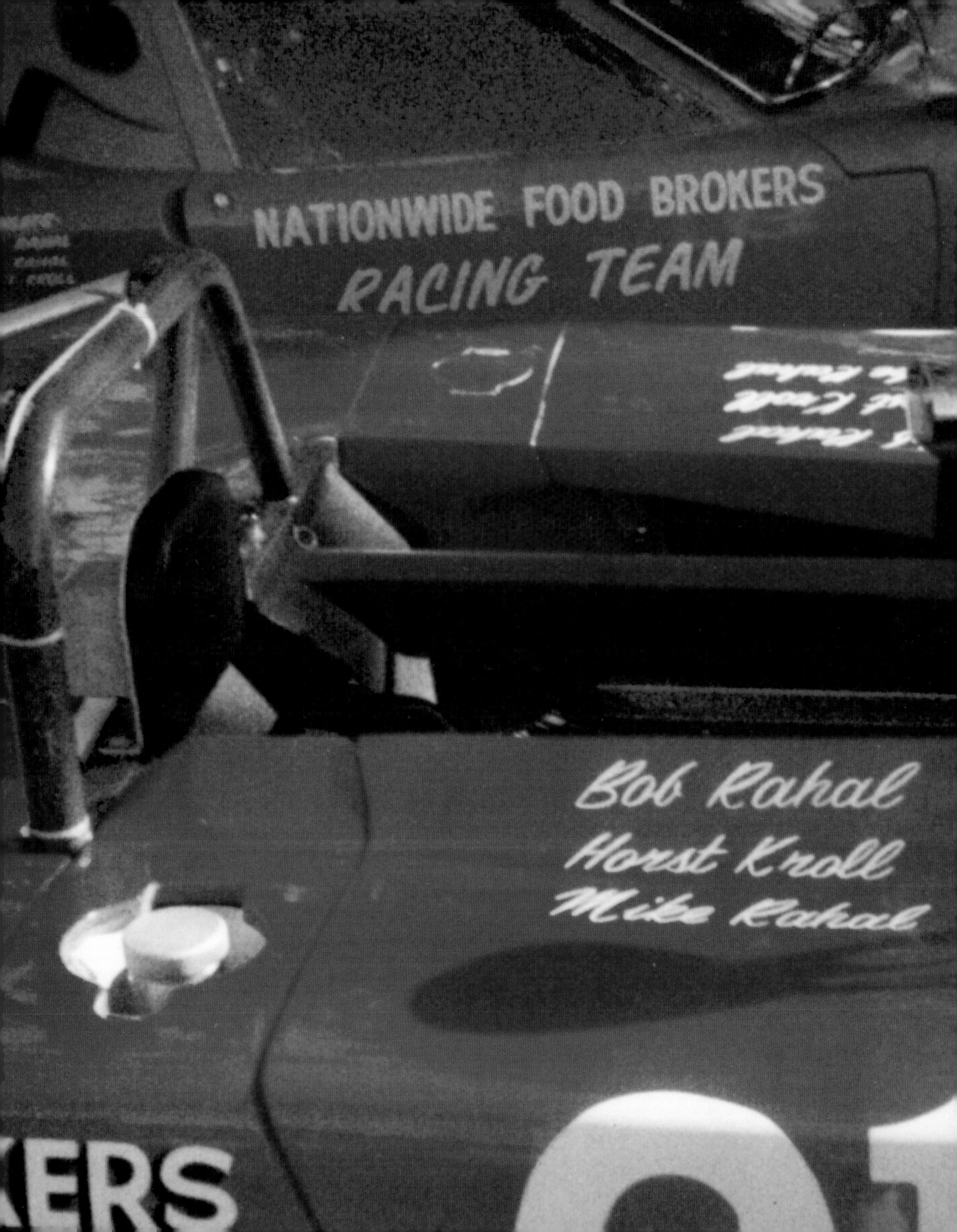
NATIONWIDE FOOD BROKERS
RACING TEAM
Bob Rahal
Horst Kroll
Mike Rahal
KERS

"Motor racing was going to be my future."

At Denison, Bobby majored in history, competed in some rallies with his BMW 2000 tii road car, and generally led the life of a Midwestern college boy. Tall and gangly, he wore his hair shaggy and long in the style of the times, although Bobby was hardly the hippie type. He joined the Phi Gamma Delta fraternity, became a popular man on campus, and enjoyed life at Denison as thoroughly and happily as his father had twenty-five years earlier.

"My dad always thought the sun rose and set over Denison," Bobby says. "At the time, I was not that interested in going there, because he had gone there, but I visited it, among other schools, and fell in love with the place." Besides history, Bobby also studied English and American literature, but felt no compelling urge to pursue any particular profession or field of study.

"I didn't really know what I wanted to do with my life," he admits. "I was totally adrift. I had been drafted in the fall of '71. I went through my draft physical and I had a bad knee, so I was disqualified. I was thinking about going to law school, but I had no burning desire

Above: Bobby (at left) and a friend, both in BMW 2002 tiis, on their way to Columbus from Denison College. "The 2002 tii, with its Kugelfischer injection system, is a very desirable car today," Mike says. "Bobby had that car all through college, and God knows how many tickets he got!" (Rahal collection)

Opposite: A detail shot of the Lola T290 cockpit shows the added name of Canadian champion Horst Kroll, who joined Mike and Bobby as a co-driver in a few long-distance races. (Rahal collection)

to be a lawyer. I didn't really want to work with my father, much to his chagrin, I'm sure, although I felt no pressure at all from him to do that."

Bobby had his share of adventures with his BMW. "The roads south, east, and north of Granville are fantastic—hilly, smooth, not much traffic. We would just go out and make our own circuits. If it took thirty minutes to do it, we'd try to do it in twenty-five, and we'd go like crazy.

"I lost my driver's license when I was eighteen. I got three tickets in one year. I look back on those days, and it was a sheer miracle that nobody got hurt or killed. One of my friends backed his 240Z through a telephone pole, sectioned the telephone pole, and ended up on the front porch of a guy's house. That was the worst thing we did.

"I became a BMW fan because of that car. I put 81,000 extremely hard miles on that thing in about three and a half years. I did an autocross in the 2000 tii in the Ohio State parking lot in 1972. That was the only time I entered that car in an official competition."

Then in the fall of 1972, Mike bought a four year-old Lotus 47, a racing version of the latest Lotus Europa road car, and the following year Bobby raced the Lotus a handful of times. He drove the Lotus in an SCCA driver's school at Mid-America Raceway in St. Louis, Missouri, in May of 1973, completing the driver's school on Saturday and racing in an SCCA regional race on Sunday. He finished second and won his class on Sunday, and had two more successful outings in the 47, winning the B/Sports racing class and finishing third overall at Blackhawk Farms Raceway in Illinois and second in class at Nelson Ledges in Ohio.

Mike and Bobby shared the Lotus, with Mike driving one weekend and Bobby the next. Father and son also raced the car in the Watkins Glen 6 Hours, with Canadian Horst Kroll co-driving. "The Lotus was a fine car, except you couldn't work on the engine without broiling your arms," Mike recalls. In the middle of 1973, Bobby convinced Mike to trade the Lotus for a newer and more powerful Lola T290.

"I was always trying to egg my father on to buy something that was a little newer and a little quicker," Bobby says. "My dad didn't have a rich father, and he had all the usual expenses and college money for us kids, but I just sat there and said, 'Spend more of your money.'"

Says Mike: "Bobby had an unbelievable talent for making you feel like it was your decision." Barbara adds: "He was already a good salesman. Let's put it that way."

Bobby ran five races with the Lola in 1973, winning two of them, and was selected by the SCCA's Chicago Region as the club's rookie of the year. The following year he drove the Lola in eight races, winning two of them and setting class track records at Mid-Ohio; Grattan; and Stuttgart, Arkansas. Bobby took the SCCA's Central Division B/Sports racing title, and at the end of 1974 he placed

After winning at Blackhawk Farms, Illinois, in July 1973, Bobby took a victory lap in the Lola T290 with his mom, Barbara, holding the flag. "The Lola T290 we bought in 1973 was probably the closest thing to a new racing car Mike ever had," Bobby observes. (Rahal collection)

Right: On a Sunday in May, 1973, Bobby drove the Lotus 47 in one of his first SCCA races at Mid-America Raceways in Wentville, Missouri. He finished second and won his class. He had completed the SCCA driver's school the day before. (Rahal collection)

Below: Bobby pilots Mike's Lotus 47 around Nelson Ledges, Ohio. "It was a great car," Mike says. "Bobby did very well with it. He competed against cars with much bigger engines, and won." (Dave Klein, Rahal collection)

Bobby stands with the Lola T290 Mike bought in 1973. Mike built the garage in the background for his racing cars. Bobby, in his Denison T-shirt, now jokes about being a "long-haired hippie" at that time. His BMW 2002 tii is parked at left. (Rahal collection)

third in the SCCA's B Sports/racing national championship at the annual Road Atlanta runoffs, behind B/SR top dogs Jerry Hansen and Mike Hall.

"It was an emotional thing for [my dad], because when I started I was Mike Rahal's son, Bob. Later, as things went along, he became Bobby Rahal's dad, Mike. As long as I stayed in school, he let me race his cars. Even though I was winning races, and that was a pretty big deal, I still had no thoughts of racing professionally."

As he slowly proved his talent as a driver, Bobby began to find the motivation and satisfaction that was lacking elsewhere in his life. "In 1973 and '74 I was really adrift as a young man. I didn't know what I wanted to do in life and, coincidentally, I started racing, and all of a sudden there was a motivation. Fortunately, there was enough success and enough assistance kept coming that I was able to continue."

Bobby also raced a Rondel FB car toward the end of 1974. By this time he was thinking more and more seriously of trying to be a professional racer. A wealthy Denison friend, Steve Uhlein, who was a member of the Schlitz Brewing family and a rabid car enthusiast, bought the Formula 2 Rondel from Ron Dennis. A few years later, Dennis went on to take over the McLaren F1 team and steer it to seven F1 World Championships. The more powerful F2 engine was replaced with a Formula Atlantic motor, and Bobby raced the car three times. He finished first in the FB class and turned the fastest lap in a pair of SCCA nationals at Indianapolis Raceway Park and Elkhart Lake, winning the FB class at IRP. Bobby then ran a professional Formula Atlantic race in September at Watkins Glen, where he qualified thirteenth and moved up to eighth before getting involved in a collision with another car driven by Bruce McGinnis.

"Because it was an F2 car, the Rondel was a little overweight, but we ran pretty well," he says. "All the hotshoes were there—guys like Bill O'Connor and Bill Brack and Tom Klausler. Until then, I didn't think I could run with them."

For the 1975 season, Uhlein and Bobby decided to sell the Rondel and roll the proceeds into the purchase of a Lola T360 Formula Atlantic car to race in the Canadian Formula Atlantic series. Bobby's first professional racing car was maintained, as were all of Mike's cars, in the garage next to the Rahal family home on Crescent Boulevard, with Wiley McCoy paid to prepare the car and run the family team.

McCoy went on to build engines for McLaren Engines in Detroit. He bought controlling interest in the company in 1998. Clay Filson, who would work for Rahal for many years, also joined the family operation, although strictly as an enthusiastic volunteer. There was also a harbinger of the future in the Red Roof Inns stickers the car carried as the result of a small amount of sponsorship from Red Roof owner Jim Trueman.

"This is my first formula car race, at Indianapolis Raceway Park, around the first week in September 1974," Bobby says. "I'm passing a Formula 5000 car here, with Mike Hall hard on my tail. I beat Mike in the Rondel and won that race." (Rahal collection)

Barbara's lap chart of Bobby's race at Blackhawk Farms. Driving the No. 61 Lola T290, Bobby led all but the penultimate lap and set a new track record on his way to victory.

"Really, my racing progress started to take hold right toward the end of my college days," Bobby says. "It became very easy to see that I needed to follow this, and with guys like Trueman and Steve Uhlein, who bought the car for me, and my dad, they made the transition easy. I'm not sure if I found racing or it found me. It all happened at the right time."

The seven-race pro Atlantic season in Canada opened in the spring, but before that Bobby ran an SCCA National at West Palm Beach in Florida as a shakedown and won easily. The first Canadian Atlantic race took place at Edmonton on a road course just outside the western Canadian city, and Bobby missed his Denison graduation ceremony because it conflicted with that all-important opening race. All the top Atlantic stars of the time were at Edmonton, racers like three-time champion Bill Brack, Tom Klausler, and twenty-three-year-old French-Canadian phenom Gilles Villeneuve. Bobby, then twenty-two, showed his talent and an aggressive style by qualifying second fastest.

The race wasn't so good, as he was stopped by an electrical failure, but he had already shown he could run with the best drivers in a hotly contested and increasingly respected series. Bobby began to think that he really could make it as a professional racing driver.

"The realization hit me at that first race at Edmonton. I went there thinking if I could get in the top ten, I'd be thrilled, but I qualified second, and the next weekend we were on pole at Westwood, and all of a sudden I started to think, 'Maybe, maybe.'"

Round two was on the difficult and dangerous Westwood road circuit just outside of Vancouver, and Bobby affirmed his talent by qualifying on the pole and finishing sixth. He was an impressive second to Gilles Villeneuve in round three at Gimli, a godforsaken airfield circuit in rural Manitoba, where the race was run in pouring rain. This was Villeneuve's first Atlantic win, coming halfway through his second year in the formula, and Bobby was anxious to beat the budding Canadian hero.

The next four races were littered with mechanical trouble, however, and Bobby failed to finish any of them. He took a distant ninth in the championship, which was won for the third straight year by forty-two-year-old Canadian veteran Brack. A few weeks after the close of the Canadian season, there was a nonchampionship race at Brainerd, Minnesota, and for the first time in months, Bobby made the finish, coming second to Brack after qualifying on the pole.

"At Brainerd, Brack and I had a racelong tussle, and I just lost out through inexperience, I think. He and I lapped everybody, Villeneuve included. The Lola was a fragile car. We had a hell of a year, and it was really from that year that I felt it was possible, that I could compete with the best."

Wiley McCoy was Bobby's chief mechanic with the family team in 1975, then moved with Bobby to Doug Shierson's team the following year. (Marc Sproule)

In the summer of 1975, Price Cobb, Bobby, and Gilles Villeneuve stand in a rainy victory ceremony after the Formula Atlantic race at Gimli in Manitoba, Canada. This was Villeneuve's career first Atlantic victory. Bobby placed second and Cobb was third. (Rahal collection)

Bobby steers the Lola T360 into a corner at Brainerd, Minnesota, on September 7, 1975. He battled hard with Bill Brack that day, finishing second to veteran Brack and beating archrival Villeneuve. (Marc Sproule)

Bobby also competed in two Super Vee races at the end of 1975 at Watkins Glen and Mosport, finishing second in both. The family team then went to the SCCA's runoffs at Road Atlanta at the end of the year with a 1974 March lent for the occasion by March distributor Doug Shierson, for whom Bobby had agreed to drive in the 1976 Atlantic series. Bobby won the race and the SCCA's Atlantic title at the runoffs and was duly awarded the President's Cup, the club's top award.

Shierson enjoyed what both he and Bobby hoped was a prelude to a strong 1976 season. "We got down there and had some silly problems with the car, something electrical," Shierson

NOVEMBER 8, 1975   AUTOWEEK   PAGE 3

AUTOWEEK SPECIAL SECTION

Bobby Rahal Best In FB; Maybe In US

Formula B is a race anticipated with a great deal of excitement. It is one of the two or three most competitive of all the SCCA classes—certainly the most closely fought of the fast classes—and it's usually one of the best events of the weekend at the Champion Classic.

FORMULA B, CHAMPION SPARK PLUG ROAD RACING CLASSIC, ROAD ATLANTA, GAINESVILLE, GEORGIA. NOVEMBER 2, 1975.

QUALIFYING TIMES
1-Jim Crawley, Frenchtown, N.J., Chevron B29, 1:22.929 for an average speed of 109.404mph; 2-Bobby Rahal, Glen Ellyn, Ill., March 75B, 1:22.938; 3-Tom Pumpelly, McLean, Va., March, 1:2.994; 4-Fred Phillips, Shreveport, La., Lola T360, 1:23.040; 5-Ken Duclos, Boxboro, Mass., Brabham BT40, 1:23.319; 6-Tom Outcault, Middletown, Ohio, March 74B, 1:23.952; 7-Jon Norman, Oakland, Calif., Lotus 69C, 1:24.142; 8-Eric Kerman, Glen Cove, N.Y., March 75B, 1:24.154; 9-Chip Mead, Dayton, Ohio, March 75B, 1:24.156; 10-Pat Walter, Novato, Calif., Ralt RT1, 1:24.610; 11-Mike Rand, Amherst, Mass., Brabham BT40, 1:24.708; 12-Joe Sposato, Ridgefield, Conn., Chevron B29, 1:25.753; 13-Bob Young, Snowmass Resort, Colo., Lola T360, 1:27.174; 14-Warren Pauge, Hacienda Hts., Calif., Brabham BT38, 1:27.896; 15-Sandy Shepard, Lake Dallas, Tex., Lola T360, 1:27.998; 16-Mike Winn, Little Rock, Ark., Merlyn Mk21, 1:28.127; 17-Steve Jizmagian, San Francisco, Calif., March 722, 1:28.519; 18-John Elder, Rosemount, Minn., Brabham BT40, 1:31.366; 19-Charlie Derbes III, Metairie, La., Brabham BT29, 1:31.540; 20-Porter Brownlee, Little Rock, Ark., Merlyn Mk21, 1:34.262.

RESULTS
1. Rahal, 18 laps or 45.6 miles in 24:54.8 minutes for an average speed of 109.43mph; 2-Crawley, 18; 3-Kerman, 18; 4-Norman, 18; 5-Mead, 18; 6-Outcault, 18; 7-Walter, 18; 8-Rand, 18; 9-Shepard, 18; 10-Pauge, 17; 11-Winn, 17; 12-Phillips, 16, (not running at finish); 13-Young, 16, (not running at finish); 14-Brownlee, 16, (not running at finish); 15-Derbes, 14, (not running at finish); 16-Duclos, 12, (not running at finish); 17-Sposato, 12, (not running at finish); 18-Jizmagian, 12.
DNF: 19-Pumpelly, 5.
DNS: 20-Elder.
WEATHER: Clear, sunny, 75 degrees.
CROWD: 30,000 est.
MARGIN OF VICTORY: 8.2 seconds
FASTEST LAP: Rahal, lap 7, 1:22.4 (new record) at 110.097mph.

The qualifying times looked promising, that's for sure. Jim Crawley held the pole at 1:22.929. Then there was a long gap—almost a hundredth of a second—to Bobby Rahal's 1:22.938. Then a full six hundredths to Tom Pumpelly and 0.04 more to Fred Phillips. Just over 11 seconds covered the whole grid of 20 cars. It should have been a hell of a race.

Should have been, but wasn't. Rahal shot off ahead of Crawley at the start, as did Pumpelly. Bobby was going as though he wanted to go home early, and he and Crawley (who repassed Pumpelly's

Young Bobby Rahal gets the Formula B winner's flag and a handshake at the Champion Classic.   *Cory Farley photo*

March) began to sprint away from Phillips in third and 1974 champ Ken Duclos. Second place was seven seconds from third by lap seven. What had happened to SCCA's plan to schedule the good races on Sunday?

The good race, it turned out, was for third place. Duclos, Eric Kerman, and Phillips had worked their respective ways into a two-car-sized patch of track and were attempting to occupy it simultaneously. It was quite a show for a couple of laps, but then Duclos came smoking into the pits and that put everything on ice.

Oh, there was one moment of excitement when Rahal got up into some traffic and Crawley closed to three or four seconds, but as soon as Bobby got clear he pulled out again. And a battle materialized for awhile when Chip Mead

started to come up on Jon Norman. Mead had only qualified ninth, but through arduous effort managed to come right up alongside Norman by halfway through the last lap. He tried hard in turn six as Rahal was taking the flag at Start/Finish and tried hard again in 11 as Crawley crossed the line for second, but couldn't quite get it either place and wound up a close fifth to Norman's fourth and Kerman's strong third.

An informal pressroom poll yielded the consensus that of all the young drivers in America today, Rahal probably has the best chance of Making It. He's only 22, he has money in the family and more money in sponsorship from Red Roof Inns, and he appears to be both absolutely fearless and at the same time possessed of enough judgement not to be reckless.

Remember, you read it in *Autoweek* first.—*Cory Farley*

Opposite: At Mosport, Bobby drove Bill Scott's Royale Super Vee in September 1975. "I raced with Bill Scott both there and at the Glen," Bobby says. "I finished second to Eddie Miller in both races." (Gemini Enterprises, Rahal collection)

Bobby sizes up the new March 76B Atlantic car at the opening of Shierson's new shop near the end of December 1976. Most of the top Atlantic drivers that year raced Marches. Lola, Chevron, and Ralt made up the rest of the field. (Rahal collection)

remembers. "It was really frustrating, but finally we got it all together and Bobby went out and nobody saw him. He was as good as, if not better than, the car that day. It was fun to watch."

In December of 1975, Bobby was the subject of a two-column story in the *New York Times*. The writer concluded his story this way: "Bobby Rahal is a name to keep in mind. He could be this country's next big hope in international racing."

By this time, it was clear Bobby was much more than an average driver, and he went racing even more seriously in 1976, driving a March for Shierson's factory team, with McCoy continuing as Bobby's engine builder. Racers at the early stages of their careers are often not paid; they are expected to bring money to the team. Often the amount of money a team requires reflects how competitive the team owner expects the driver to be. A competitive driver would not be expected to provide as much money as an uncompetitive driver. Because Shierson felt Bobby had a good shot at the championship, Bobby didn't need to bring in a lot. By using his own engines from the previous year, and with financial help from Mike and Jim Trueman, Bobby put together his program. Shierson's family was the Marathon Oil distributor for the Midwest, and Doug raced 2-liter sports cars successfully and became March's North American distributor before running a winning Indy car team from 1983 through 1991.

"Mike and I used to race 2-liter cars against each other. That's how it all started," Shierson says about his agreement with Bobby for 1976. "Really, it came down, I think, to the friendship with Mike and Barbara. When Bobby started racing in Formula Atlantic, we were running pretty successfully in Atlantic, and I had the March deal. Mike talked to us, and we said we'd run Bobby, and he said he wanted to bring Wiley McCoy with him to do the engines. That, I'm afraid, was only semi-successful, because there were a number of engine failures that really cut down on Bobby's performance that year, which was too bad, because in all honesty, that year he was quicker than Gilles."

Bobby had also talked to Kris Harrison about joining Harrison's Ecurie Canada team, which ended up running archrival Villeneuve in 1976. Bobby had preferred Ecurie Canada because he admired team manager Ray Wardell, who had run the factory March F2 team in 1974 and 1975, and was also involved with March's F1 effort. Wardell was a sharp, well-connected man who nurtured Villeneuve's talent and later founded Pi Electronics, one of the foremost suppliers of onboard data and electronic systems to the racing industry.

Bobby started the 1976 season at Sebring, where he co-drove a Chevy Monza GT car with Jim Trueman in the 12 Hours. Bobby qualified in the top ten, but the car was brand-new and wasn't really ready for a long-distance race. Bobby and Trueman retired early with a series of mechanical problems.

The focus then shifted back to Formula Atlantic. Driving for Shierson's professional team with his car sponsored by Swing, an orange drink, Bobby was impressive as he battled at or near the front of the field with champion-to-be Villeneuve and top Atlantic drivers of the time like three-time champion Brack, Tom Klausler, Bertil Roos, Elliott Forbes-Robinson, Tom Gloy, Marty Loft, Howdy Holmes, and Price Cobb. But Bobby was entirely luckless, hitting trouble in almost every race except for Mosport near the end of the year, where he won handily. Archrival Villeneuve didn't race at Mosport, however, because of a shortage of sponsorship even after he had already wrapped up both IMSA's American and the Canadian Automobile Sport Club (CASC) Canadian Atlantic titles.

"I'm absolutely convinced that if Gilles had been at Mosport, he never would have seen Bobby," Shierson declares. "Bobby was in a league of his own. I know Bobby felt he would have beaten Gilles that day. Mosport stands out from that year because it was such a disappointment that Gilles wasn't there."

Other than that lone victory without Villeneuve, Bobby had only a single third, a fourth, and a couple of fifths, finishing sixth and seventh in each championship. "I was always very disap-

Bobby's first year with a professional team was 1976, with Doug Shierson (at right). His was one of five cars run by Shierson's Adrian, Michigan-based team. As part of the deal, Bobby had to supply his own engines, which he had run in the 1975 season. (Rahal collection)

Rahal shakes bad luck wins final Player's race

MOSPORT —— Bobby Rahal came out from under his little black cloud at Mosport yesterday.

Rahal, 23, of Chicago, won the final race of the Player's Challenge Series for the Canadian Driving Championship, ending what had been a frustrating season until yesterday.

Generally regarded as one of the best young drivers in the U.S., Rahal has been left in the dust by new Canadian driving champion Gilles Villeneuve of Berthierville, Que., this season.

It wasn't that Rahal was that slow; it was that little problems kept cropping up on his March Formula Atlantic car, putting him on the sidelines or slowing him down so much that he rarely could stay close to Villeneuve.

"I started to ask myself, 'what have I done to deserve this? I wish that little black cloud over my head would get away from me,'" Rahal said.

Yesterday was pure sunshine in comparison.

Rahal took the lead from Tom Klausler of Pallatine, Ill., on the seventh lap of the 41-lap (100-mile) race and had no trouble staying in front to win by a comfortable 32 seconds over Tom Gloy of Walnut Creek, Calif., in a Tui.

Klausler blew an engine trying to stay in front of Rahal. thus ending any possibility of a close race for first.

Rahal's victory was only slightly less satisfying because neither Villeneuve nor former Canadian champ Bill Brack of Toronto was in it.

Villeneuve ran out of money when his sponsor went bankrupt, and Brack missed the race when his STP Special ran into a mysterious electrical problem that his mechanics couldn't find.

"I don't think it would have mattered today even if they had been in it," said Rahal. "Gilles would have made it tough, but we were about a second faster than Brack. The car was handling better than it ever has.

"It was easy winning it. This was the first race that everything went just right."

Bertil Roos of Sweden, driving a Ralt, was third, with Price Cobb of Dallas, Texas, fourth in March, the only other car on the same lap with Rahal.

The top Canadian was Bruce Jensen of Newcastle, Ont., in a Chevron, finishing in fifth place, one lap down.

Marcel Talbot of Granby, Que., was seventh, helping to earn him rookie-of-the-year honors.

Pit patter: Gilles Villeneuve was on hand yesterday to collect his trophy and new Datsun F10, part of the prize for winning the Canadian driving title. He was also named series driver-of-the-year after winning four of the six races . . . Villeneuve's mechanic, Andy Roe, collected a new set of tools and a week in the Bahamas as mechanic of the year in the series . . . Talbot and Villeneuve also got a trip to the Bahamas . . . It was the final race in the series this year and the final one under Player's sponsorship. The company has announced withdrawal from the series next year.

23ᵈ Aug. 1976 —Len Coates

TV RADIO LOG

TELEVISION

8 p.m.—Channel 9, Toronto vs. Montreal, CFL Football.

8 p.m.—Channel 17, Tennis: Singles and doubles final in Canadian Open.

8:30 p.m.—Channel 7, 11, Baseball: St. Louis vs. Cincinnati, National League.

10 p.m.—Channel 3, 5, Tennis: Men's singles final, Canadian Open.

RADIO

7:45 p.m.—CFRB 1010, Toronto vs. Montreal, CFL Football.

10:15 p.m.—CKFH 1430 and CKQS-FM 99.4, Montreal vs. Los Angeles, National League Baseball.

pointed that together we couldn't have come up with a much better performance, because we should have," says Shierson."

"That was kind of a bad year," Bobby says. "We were very competitive but didn't finish many races. We did win Mosport, but we had so many stupid things happen, and, of course, Gilles won just about everything. Even some of the races that he wasn't leading he ended up winning. He was strong, but everything went his way."

Bobby scored a dominant win in the last Atlantic championship race on August 20, 1976, at Mosport. Villeneuve didn't take part in the race, which frustrated Bobby and Shierson because both believe Bobby would have beaten the great Gilles had Villeneuve been in the field. (Marc Sproule)

Villeneuve was in his third year in Formula Atlantic in 1976 and won nine of fourteen races, as well as both American and Canadian championships. This set him on the fast track toward a legendary Formula One career with Ferrari, while Bobby had just a single win and nothing much else to brag about.

"I was shattered," Bobby explains. "I mean, '76 was supposed to be my year. You know, I was the hot young guy in '75, and everybody said, 'Oh, this is your year.' Shierson's team was the factory March team, and we were supposed to have it all, but it was just one disaster after another. By the end of the year, I had so little confidence, and I just couldn't see, you know, wasting my life at trying to be a racing driver.

"I've seen guys almost—but not quite—make it, and all they did was waste their youth. Racing is, figuratively speaking, littered with the corpses of people who squandered their entire youth—in some cases inherited money, you name it—all chasing this dream. So I just bagged it. At the end of '76, I retired. I quit."

Despite a careful drive, Bobby spun off in the pouring rain at the challenging and dangerous Westwood road circuit on the outskirts of Vancouver, British Columbia. Marty Loft, a Northwest Formula Ford champion and one of Bobby's teammates, won that day, beating Villeneuve. (Marc Sproule)

The North American Formula Atlantic season opened at Long Beach, California, in April 1978. Bobby qualified on the pole but suffered a puncture just after the start. After stopping for a new tire, he stormed through the field, turned the race's fastest lap, and got up to third place before a driveshaft broke and ended his day. (Bob Tronolone)

"I could compete with anybody."

For five months Bobby attempted to pursue a more traditional career at a Chicago advertising agency. "He was working at Young and Rubicam, and all of sudden decided he couldn't stand it and had to get back to racing," Barbara remembers. "His father was not in favor of it at all." Mike agrees: "Our business was really bubbling along, and I said, 'I don't object to your racing. But you can't make this into a living.'"

At a family reunion in Cleveland early in 1977, Bobby and Mike engaged in the only argument they ever had about racing. "I was going to get paid $18,000 for racing that year," Bobby says, "and he said I could come to work for him and he'd pay me $18,000 a year, and stop trying to be a professional racing driver. That's the only time I ever remember him saying to me, 'You're wasting your time. Maybe you ought to be doing something else.'"

There was method to Bobby's madness, however, because an offer had materialized from Wall Street bond trader Jim Morgan for Bobby to join his new Atlantic team. Morgan had raced Atlantic cars as an SCCA amateur and wanted to try his hand at the pro series. He had bought a couple of 1976 Marches from Ecurie Canada that had been raced by Gilles Villeneuve and asked Shierson for advice on setting up his team. Among other things, Shierson suggested to Morgan that he hire Rahal as a teammate to win races for the team and teach Morgan the finer points of driving and racing.

Above: After quitting racing for five months in the winter of 1976 and 1977, Bobby decided to give it another try and was actually paid to drive in 1977 by bond broker and amateur racer Jim Morgan. "We ran at the SCCA National at the Texas World Speedway to shake down the cars before the pro season," Bobby says. (Rahal collection)

Above: Bobby hurries Jim Morgan's March around the tight road course in Shubenacadie, Nova Scotia, just outside of Halifax. Electrical trouble ended his race. (Marc Sproule)

Right: The professional Atlantic season opened in March at Mosport. Seconds after the start, Keke Rosberg puts two wheels in the grass inside Gilles Villeneuve and Price Cobb, with Bobby in fourth ahead of Tom Gloy. "I wrote off one car in practice when the wing broke," Bobby remembers. (Marc Sproule)

Shierson remembers a conversation earlier that winter with Bobby. "I called him and told him, 'You can't do this. You can't quit,' " Shierson recalls. " 'You've got so much talent,' I told him. 'You will succeed. Believe me, you have to have the faith.' He was young, and terribly disappointed after the '76 season. It was probably a good thing that he did go take a break because it refocused him and made him realize how much he missed it. "

Recounts Bobby: "Doug asked if I was interested in talking to Jim Morgan, and I'll always remember my first wife, Lori, said, 'You're never going to forgive yourself if you don't give it a go.' "

Bobby and Lori lived together for much of 1976 and were married in March of 1977. A promising graphic artist, Lori was a strong supporter of Bobby's racing, but the stress of him trying to build a career in racing eventually tore the marriage apart.

"It was a whirlwind relationship and marriage" Bobby says. "We were very young. I was twenty-four and Lori was twenty-two. Lori had a strong desire to build a career in advertising and today is a group manager for a studio in Chicago. She's a very talented person, and the idea of subverting that desire to follow me around I think lost favor over time.

"I look back and think how grown-up we thought we were and how childlike we were, and also how many expectations there were for us and how unrealistic they were. It was a real shame because I think we were victims of youth and, in some respects, the racing culture. More than anything, though, it was the unrealistic demands we made of each other that led to the dissolution of the marriage."

Driving one of Morgan's year-old Marches, the newly married Rahal was supercompetitive in 1977, battling wheel to wheel with defending champion Villeneuve and Atlantic newcomer Keke Rosberg, who later won the 1982 F1 World Championship. Bobby won at Gimli and looked ready to win again in the year's last race in Quebec City. Morgan bought Rahal a new Ralt for that race, and Bobby appeared to have the race in the bag, holding a small lead over Villeneuve until a plug lead fell off. He had to stop at the pits to reattach the errant wire, and he rejoined to finish a strong second to the great Gilles, who wrapped up his second straight Atlantic title that day.

Bobby finished the year second to Villeneuve in the championship, beating three-time champion Brack and the fiercely aggressive Rosberg. His results proved that Lori and Shierson had been right to push him back into racing, and with Morgan's support, a fresh effort was planned to win the 1978 Formula Atlantic title.

Bobby spent the month of January racing in five Formula Atlantic races in New Zealand, paired for the first and only time in his career with Keke Rosberg on Fred Opert's team. Bobby brought with him engines from Jim Morgan Racing, sponsorship from Mike's company, Hartog, and five sets of tires that he took on the plane as personal luggage, given to him by Goodyear's racing director, Leo Mehl. "One of the bluest times of my life was when I spent Christmas having dinner at the L.A. airport restaurant," he says.

After placing second in two of the five races and finishing third in the championship, behind winner Rosberg and Larry Perkins, Bobby flew home in a confident frame of mind. Bobby's North American Atlantic car was run in 1978 by Oregonian Pierre Phillips's team, still with sponsorship from Jim Morgan. There was some additional sponsorship from old friend Jim Trueman's Red Roof Inns, and Bobby drove one of the new Ralt RT1s with which he had almost beaten Villeneuve in the last race of 1977.

This is the official reprimand Bobby received from Canadian Automobile Sports Car Club stewards for riding back to the pits atop Gilles Villeneuve's car after his own car broke during qualifying.

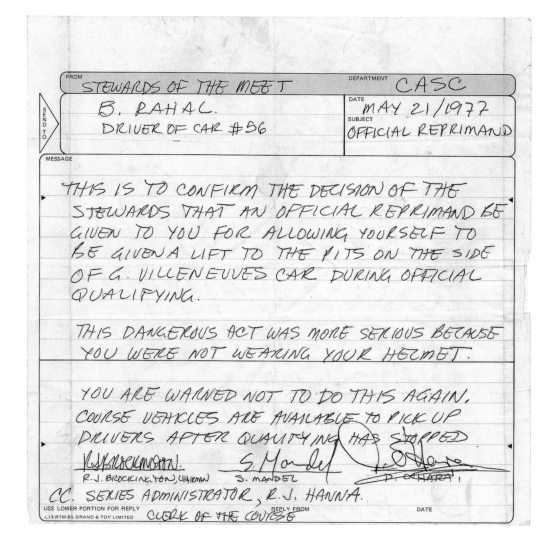

FROM STEWARDS OF THE MEET   DEPARTMENT CASC

SEND TO   B. RAHAL. DRIVER OF CAR #56   DATE MAY 21/1977   SUBJECT OFFICIAL REPRIMAND

MESSAGE

THIS IS TO CONFIRM THE DECISION OF THE STEWARDS THAT AN OFFICIAL REPRIMAND BE GIVEN TO YOU FOR ALLOWING YOURSELF TO BE GIVEN A LIFT TO THE PITS ON THE SIDE OF G. VILLENEUVES CAR DURING OFFICIAL QUALIFYING.

THIS DANGEROUS ACT WAS MORE SERIOUS BECAUSE YOU WERE NOT WEARING YOUR HELMET.

YOU ARE WARNED NOT TO DO THIS AGAIN. COURSE VEHICLES ARE AVAILABLE TO PICK UP DRIVERS AFTER QUALIFYING HAS STOPPED

R.J. BROCKINGTON, CHAIRMAN   S. MANDEL   D. O'HARA

CC. SERIES ADMINISTRATOR, R.J. HANNA.

USE LOWER PORTION FOR REPLY   REPLY FROM   DATE
L13-RTM-8½ GRAND & TOY LIMITED   CLERK OF THE COURSE

Glen Ellyn's Rahal racing driver on the move

"A good car, the right age to start, sensational driving ability — it all looks good for Bobby Rahal. Remember the name."

—Autoweek

By Bruce Shapin

DON'T SHED ANY tears for Bobby Rahal. He isn't a second-rate driver trying to earn a name for himself; he's one of the fastest rising stars in the complicated world of auto racing.

That's right. Bobby Rahal, a lifelong resident of Glen Ellyn and a '71 graduate of Glenbard West, has been climbing up the ladder to racing stardom, seeking his No. 1 goal-Formula 1.

He's racing in the Labatt Challenge Series for Formula Atlantic cars and in the Can-Am Series this year. Picking up some important exposure and an occasional victory while he serves his apprenticeship on the track. Rahal is in second place in the Labatt point standings.

"Most people in racing will tell you that Formula Atlantic is the most competitive series in the world," said Rahal during a rare stopover in Glen Ellyn. "Formula Atlantic cars are the training ground for Formula 1 and Indy type cars."

LABELED "THE next Mario Andretti" by the racing press, Rahal is anxious to get his chance in Formula 1. But he also knows that most American drivers don't get that opportunity until their late '20s.

"That's one of the bad parts of being an American driver," said Rahal. "Most of the European drivers get a sponsor in Formula 1 cars when they're my age [Bobby is 24], but the American driver has to wait while he searches for financial backing to keep racing until the opportunity comes up.

"Motor racing works on the assumption that you're good and you have the financial ability to keep going. That's the way it is."

Rahal's Formula Atlantic car is sponsored by James Morgan of New York, but he's still searching for financial help on the Can-Am circuit. Morgan provides Rahal with a team, car, and everything else he needs. Rahal is paid a salary and gets a percentage of his winnings.

SO FAR this season Rahal has earned more than $25,000 in prize money. His biggest payday came June 26 when he captured Labatt's Manitoba Challenge race in his Formula Atlantic. Rahal had trouble at the start of the race ["The track was damp and the first three rows spun out in the first turn"], but he recovered in time and worked his way up to the lead.

"I was in 16th place when I got back on the track," he said. "I just took my time and started working up gradually till I took the lead." Rahal became the leader with 17 laps left, holding off several charges to capture

Rahal: 'the next Mario Andretti'

the title by three seconds.

"The cars are so equal that it comes down to driver ability," Rahal added. At Manitoba the difference between the pole car and the last row was a little more than two seconds after time trials."

This year Bobby has entered nine races throughout Canada and the United States, traveling to each one in a motor home with his wife, Lori. This weekend he'll be in New York testing some chassis modifications on the Formula Atlantic car. Then it's up to Nova Scotia, a few more races, the Labatt finale through the streets of Quebec City

Please turn to page 62

Rahal stands second in Can Am's Labatt point standings.

The expanded series opened at Long Beach, the first time Atlantic cars raced at Chris Pook's classic California street race, and Bobby was sharp and ready for the new season. Bobby qualified on the pole in Long Beach, only to be bumped on the pace lap by a driver on the second row, cutting a tire so that he had to stop at the pits and start the race dead last. He stormed through the field, however, turned the fastest lap, and got up to third before being stopped for good by a broken drive shaft.

That showing earned Bobby a lot of recognition, including a special award for the performance of the race from Austro-Canadian Walter Wolf, who ran a Formula One team with Jody Scheckter as the driver. Bobby was introduced to Wolf by his publicist Rod Campbell, whose company now handles all of Ford's racing public relations work. Wolf invited Bobby to drive some Formula Three races in Europe, scheduled around his Atlantic commitments in the United States and Canada. Wolf was a partner with commodities broker Oliver Stahel in a Formula Three team, using cars built by fledgling Italian manufacturer Dallara. Bobby flew

During January 1978, Bobby was teamed with Keke Rosberg in the five-race New Zealand Atlantic series. Here he drives one of Fred Opert's Chevrons at Pukekohe, New Zealand, where he finished second. Opert supplied the chassis and Bobby had to bring his own supply of engines and tires from the U.S. (D. Lewry/Rahal collection)

61

Above: At the Long Beach season-opener in April Bobby leads the Formula Atlantic field into the first turn on the pace lap. Howdy Holmes is alongside. Moments later Eje Elgh (5) hit Bobby and punctured his rear tire. (Bob Tronolone)

Right: Bobby made his Formula Three debut in Monaco driving Walter Wolf's Dallara. When the F3 series traveled to Germany three weeks later, Bobby learned the legendary 14-mile Nurburgring circuit (shown here) well enough to finish third on his first visit. (Rahal collection)

to Italy to test the car for his first taste, from the cockpit, of European racing.

"I showed up at the Milan airport, and I was picked up by a fellow named Gordon Horne, who I didn't know from Adam, who was the team manager," Bobby tells the story. "We go to Varano, and I'm put up at the local hotel. Nobody speaks any English there, and I don't speak any Italian, but they knew I was there with the race team, which was all the reason in the world for them to be generous to me, and it was a wonderful experience.

"With gesturing and pointing, I got by and was really made to feel at home. The first time I got in the car, the team tied a rope behind a Fiat 500 and towed me through town. That was the way we got to the track, rain or shine.

"Then we got to this little track and started warming up, and there were maybe ten or twenty people out there, and after an hour you'd see fifty or a hundred people, and pretty soon there were three or four hundred of them. The whole village was out there, watching me go around and around. It was so foreign from anything I'd ever experienced. Here I was, just a little Formula Three guy, and it made me feel something special. I really loved racing in Europe."

In May, at no less a place than Monaco, Bobby made his European racing debut. It was an impressive start too, as Bobby qualified third and led his qualifying heat before spinning twice because of a sticking gearbox. Even so, he recovered to finish fourth behind Teo Fabi, Derek Warwick, and Elio de Angelis, all of whom went on to race F1 cars and were the top F3 drivers of those days. In the final, Bobby moved up quickly and was running fifth when he clipped a curb

At Nurburgring Bobby shares the podium with second-place finisher Patrick Gaillard and Jan Lammers (not in the photo), who won the race. That Bobby placed third was remarkable because his Dallara was outpaced by other cars on much of the track. Bobby explains: "When we were timed, I was fastest through one series of corners, but the car was second *slowest* on the straight-aways." (Rahal collection)

and bent his suspension, ending his race. But he had shown he could run with the top Europeans on their turf, even though the Dallara wasn't entirely the equal of the Ralts and Chevrons driven by almost everyone else. Three weeks later Bobby again looked good, finishing third at the Nurburgring in Germany before some structural problems appeared in the Dallara chassis.

"We did real well at the Nurburgring, but I guess the 'Ring wore the chassis right out," Bobby grins at the story. " After the Nurburgring, we went to Dijon in France, and the car was horrible. It was broken in half, basically, so we didn't even start the race. All the rivets had pulled out of the bulkheads and all the wheels were cracked. It's a miracle we didn't get hurt in that thing."

The car was taken back to Dallara and completely rebuilt in time for the European championship race at Monza at the end of June, known as the Grand Premio Della Lotteria.

The victory celebration after the New Zealand Grand Prix at Pukekohe. Keke Rosberg (right) won the race, Bobby was second, Larry Perkins (left) was third, and David Oxton (far left) was fourth. Oxton and Perkins were Australians who both raced in Europe, and Perkins raced in F1 before becoming one of his country's top touring car racers. (Marshall Photographic/Rahal collection)

Bobby leads the opening lap at Quebec City in June, chased
by Keke Rosberg, Price Cobb, and Jeff Wood. Rosberg and
Bobby tangled, which knocked Bobby out of the race and
banged up his hand when the impact wrenched the
steering wheel from his grip. (Marc Sproule)

Bobby was an impressive second in his qualifying heat at Monza and finished sixth in the final before flying back to the States to score a resounding win in an Atlantic race at Connecticut's Lime Rock Park on July Fourth. It was his first entirely trouble-free race of the year, and his first and only win of 1978 on home soil.

Back in Europe, Bobby was crashed out but entirely uninjured in a huge, multicar wreck at the start of the F3 race supporting the British GP. "That accident was actually caused by [Nelson] Piquet," Bobby recalls. "He came across everybody, and all hell broke loose. That was quite a famous accident."

He finished third in the next two Atlantic races run at Road America and a one-time-only street race in Hamilton, Ontario. Bobby's first European season came to an end in August with a third place and the fastest lap at the Osterreichring in Austria. He then returned home for the last two races of the Atlantic season in Canada at Three Rivers and Montreal.

"I commuted back and forth all year," Bobby says. "I was living in Connecticut and had an apartment in Parma, Italy. We didn't get many results out of that year, but it was a great year. I really enjoyed it. We ran strong and led a lot in Atlantic. We were leading at Westwood, and the car broke. We won at Lime Rock and we were leading at Montreal, and the car overheated because a bunch of leaves got stuck in the radiator opening."

A lot of talk was going on with Wolf about Bobby driving one of Wolf's F1 cars in 1979, starting with a pair of experimental outings in the last two Grand Prix races of 1978 at Watkins Glen and Montreal. "If things went well, Wolf would run a two-car team in '79 and I would drive the second car," Bobby says.

Above: In 1978 the Dallara chassis was not equal to the cars built by Ralt, Chevron, or March. Though the Dallara steered well on low-speed circuits like Monaco, it had a weakness in the way the engine mounted to the chassis that affected high-speed handling. (Michael C. Brown)

Left: Bobby controls a slide as he leads the September Atlantic race on the new Ile Notre Dame circuit. Leaves got caught in his radiator, which caused his engine to overheat and ended his run. This was the very first race on the Montreal track that would host the following month's Canadian G.P. (Marc Sproule)

The performance of the Wolf F1 car presented Bobby with a steep learning curve. Compared with the roughly 200 HP he was used to in Formula Atlantic and F3, the Wolf's 3-liter Cosworth-Ford V-8 produced around 485 HP and staggering acceleration. The F1 car also had wider tires that generated considerably higher cornering and braking forces.

Bobby tested the Wolf F1 car at Brands Hatch, England, before making his F1 debut at the Glen in that year's United States East Grand Prix. Competing with a field of superstars that included World Champions Mario Andretti, James Hunt, Emerson Fittipaldi, and Niki Lauda, Bobby qualified twentieth and finished a steady twelfth, one lap behind. Argentinian Carlos Reutemann won for Ferrari. "We had kind of a tentative first race at Watkins Glen," Bobby recalls. "I think I was within a second of Scheckter in a very difficult car, the WR5, which was basically a truck. In the race, looking back, I wasn't ready for that level at that point in time, but we stayed out of trouble and finished."

In Montreal the following weekend at the first F1 race on Ile Notre Dame in the middle of the Saint Lawrence River, Bobby was determined to try harder. A few weeks earlier he had led the Atlantic race on the same track, a test race to make sure the track was ready for its debut F1 race. So Bobby had the advantage of some track time over his new rivals.

"I was a little bit more comfortable in the car in Montreal," Bobby says. "It was raining, and at one point we were up to fifth quickest with not too much time to go. I wanted to show everybody how good I was and I ended up sliding off the road and taking a corner off. The way the car was manufactured, it tore the pick-up points off and the car was irreparable."

Wolf's team retrieved one of its previous year's cars that had been on display at the downtown Hyatt Hotel to help promote the race. The show car was turned overnight into a racing car, and Bobby qualified twentieth once again, starting the race beside 1976 World Champion James Hunt.

"To the credit of the Wolf people and their sense of obligation to Oliver," Bobby says, "they dragged the WR1 out and prepared it to qualify and, I think against all expectations, I qualified it. I don't think people thought we were going to make it go, but I think in some respects it was the car to have. It was the car in which Scheckter had done so well at Monaco and Long Beach the year before. It put the power down well and was a nimble little car. It wasn't a ground-effect car, which the WR5 was."

Bobby made a great start, passing four cars on the opening lap and getting up to eleventh place after just nine laps. "I was right behind Patrick Tambay in one of the McLarens and was looking for a way past him, and then the flapper valve in the fuel system started sticking open. You'd go into a corner and all the fuel would run out of the tank and it would misfire."

Below: At Montreal, Bobby was anxious to show his speed, and he was fifth quickest in practice before he pushed a little too hard in the rain and crashed minutes after this picture was taken. The car was heavily damaged and could not be repaired that weekend. (LAT Photographic)

Opposite: Bobby accelerates the WR5 up the hill through the esses at the Glen. "The car was horrible," Bobby says. "The steering was extremely heavy, and the car felt ponderous. Even Scheckter had a hard time making the thing work." He drove steadily to finish twelfth. (LAT Photographic)

Bobby impressed in the race, and moved quickly through the field. Here he leads Keke Rosberg, Didier Pironi, James Hunt, and Jacques Laffite. But after just sixteen laps, his race ended when a fuel-related misfire could not be cured in the pits. (LAT Photographic)

The misfire got worse, and Bobby had to stop at the pits for attention. Various cures were tried but it turned out that the rubber valve had stiffened and become inoperable because the car had spent too many days sitting on show. After only sixteen laps, Bobby's second and last F1 race was over. "We ended up not finishing, but I felt really pretty proud of the performance," Bobby says.

Famously, the race was won by Gilles Villeneuve, who scored his first F1 victory that day in his home province, beating Bobby's teammate, Scheckter, and Villeneuve's own Ferrari teammate, Reutemann.

The day after the Canadian GP, in a meeting with Wolf F1 team manager, Peter Warr, Bobby felt his hopes of a full-time F1 drive with Wolf in 1979 beginning to slip away. "I remember sitting in a hotel the next day in Montreal with Rod Campbell and Peter Warr, and Peter told me that if I was lucky they would hire me for next year. He was very noncommittal, and I sort of felt like Damocles's sword was hanging over my head. I was either going to be anointed or I was going to be dead.

"Peter Warr was very cold, very matter of fact," Bobby adds. "He had no room, or time, for sentimentality or emotion. In some respects I got the idea that he had fulfilled his obligations to Walter and Oliver, and enough was enough."

Bobby was right. The possible 1979 F1 deal with Wolf soon evaporated. Jody Scheckter left Wolf to join Ferrari, with whom he would win the 1979 World Championship, while James Hunt replaced Scheckter, moving from McLaren to Wolf. Hunt wanted a one-car team focused entirely on him.

"James had won the World Championship in '76, but two years later things had not gone well. He was obviously unhappy in a lot of respects with his life, and it affected his driving," Bobby comments. "Basically, Hunt came in, and the way I understood it, he said, 'It's a one-car deal, or I'm not here.' I was expendable.

"I felt I had shown that I could compete with anybody in Formula Three in less than equal equipment, and there were times in Formula Atlantic when I outran Gilles Villeneuve and Keke Rosberg, guys that were very well thought of. But to an American, F1 was an extremely closed society. The opportunities were very, very few and, in effect, I was finally told there was no room for me at Wolf."

Looking back, Bobby says his failure to pursue a Formula One drive more professionally is the one regret of his career. "To me, you made it to Formula One because of your talent, not because you had a bagful of money, and I didn't have that anyway. When I look back now, twenty years later, I was twenty-five when I ran F1, and I was awfully young. I had no adult supervision. Today young guys have managers and so forth, but in those days you pretty much did things on your own. Rod Campbell helped as much as he could, but it was still a different situation.

"The end result was the thing that had been my dream, to be in Formula One, I had achieved, but I had not achieved it with the degree of consistency I was hoping to," Bobby says. "Not achieving more in Formula One was a great disappointment to me, and still is to a large degree. But in my heart and mind I felt that, given the right opportunity, I could have competed with anybody in Formula One. And I guess that's all you can ask for."

LARRY SICINSKI SPORTS EDITOR

Rahal earmarked for Formula One

THE MAN WHO will follow the footsteps of Canada's Gilles Villeneuve from Formula Atlantic racing to the bigtime Grand Prix circuit next season won his first race at 17 years of age.

It was only a beginner's race at Mosport, but it was his debut. His father, Michael, who took up racing as a summertime hobby, offered him the shot behind the wheels.

BOBBY RAHAL

"If I remember correctly, it scared me half to death," said Bobby Rahal of Greenwich, Conn., runner-up to Villeneuve in 1977 and seventh on the Atlantic circuit this year after last week's third-place finish at Elkhart Lake.

He didn't race for three years after that, but took up the sport seriously in 1974. He joined the Players' circuit in 1975 and has been racing Atlantic since that time.

Why? "Just being able to do something that so few people can do for whatever reasons. And do it best," said Rahal, 25, an aggressive individual who isn't happy unless he's competing.

"I don't think it is different than any other sport. It is a glamorous thing... foreign to people in general because so few people do it — the uniqueness of it appeals to me.

"And there certainly is an ego thing involved in being able to do something better... it is mainly just a love of racing, competing and trying to make a car go as fast as it possibly can go for the longest time."

Danger, according to Rahal, who is married, is an over-rated incentive for race drivers and something people mis-read into the sport.

Safety improvements

"No one likes to get hurt. No one likes to die.. motor racing appears to be quite dangerous, but it is quite a safe sport in reality. The care and equipment you use these days is second to none and the safety of drivers has improved 1,000 per cent in the last 10 years."

Rahal, the pole sitter in three of the five Labatt's races, has probably been the fastest of all Atlantic drivers this season. Even when the member of the Red Roof Inns-Morgan Racing team hasn't had the pole, he's been in the lead and in position to win. But Lady Luck forced his Ralt RT1 into pits and out of the race three times.

Rahal changed the trend with a seven-second victory over points-leader Howdy Holmes of Ann Arbor in the fourth race at Limerock, Conn. It marked the first time anyone has come on to win a Labatt's race, starting seventh on the grid.

On the upcoming Hamilton race, Rahal said: "A street race, like the one in Hamilton, takes a great deal of precision... if you make a mistake, you hit a wall.

"You'll see good close racing. There will always be a group fighting for position. That's what makes this type of racing more enjoyable because it never becomes a procession."

Dream come true

Rahal's second-place Formula Atlantic finish last year has helped give him a shot at Formula One racing — the dream of every Atlantic driver.

As part of Canadian financier Walter Wolf's racing machine, Rahal has been chosen to pilot a second car for Wolf on the Formula One circuit next season. He will be the second half of a two-driver team, featuring Villeneuve. Ferrari, who Villeneuve is driving for this season, has traded the Bertierville, Que., native to Wolf for South African Jody Scheckter.

Rahal has been driving Formula Three (considered a step below Formula One in Europe) for Wolf, which has taken him to Europe six times since April. The American has responded with a second at Monaco, third at Nurburgring, Germany, and a near third at Monza, until an accident forced him out of the race near the finish.

Naturally, Rahal is excited about Grand Prix. But he still has his eyes set on a Formula Atlantic championship, the likes of which could come about with a first in Hamilton.

"What should I do?"

After the Wolf F1 deal vanished, Bobby decided to focus his efforts for 1979 entirely on Europe. He determined that he would move up to Formula Two, a more powerful version of both F3 and Atlantic, and worked out an agreement with car builder Chevron to compete in the twelve-round European F2 Championship. Chevron had won a number of F2 races the year before and had had success with drivers Derek Daly and Keke Rosberg. The car was run from the Chevron factory in northern England. Bobby, along with Lori, moved to Southport in Lancashire on England's northwest coast. They rented a house to be close to the Chevron factory. To Lori, Bobby's talent and commitment to racing were obvious. Separation for months on end or traveling back and forth across the Atlantic were not attractive options, so she gave up her job at William Morrow in New York to support him and travel Europe together.

"Obviously, I wanted to go back to Europe to race, and I agreed to give Chevron $100,000, which was considerably less than what March wanted for their factory ride," Bobby says. "I remember I made the phone call about four o'clock in the morning from

Above: Bobby finished fourth in the May 13, 1979, race at Vallelunga, a classic European road circuit in Italy. He was beginning to realize that the Chevron was outdated compared with the new ground-effect cars from March and Ralt. (Rahal collection)

Opposite: Bobby sits in the Chevron during practice at Thruxton, England, while the crew debriefs him. The car's bodywork is at the left. Though Chevron had a successful 1978 season, its cars were outclassed by the superior aerodynamics of the Marches and Ralts in 1979. (Michael C. Brown)

THE GOODYEAR TIRE & RUBBER COMPANY
AKRON, OHIO 44316

DIRECTOR
RACING

January 4, 1979
HLM/2

Mr Bobby Rahal
121 East Middle Patent
Greenwich, CT   06830

Dear Bobby:

Thank you for the Christmas present. I hope your
progress continues as well next year as it has gone
this year.

You're certain to become a famous race driver one
of these days.

Sincerely,

H L Mehl
cla

Above: Goodyear's racing boss Leo Mehl sent this letter of encouragement to Bobby at the beginning of 1979.

Right: Cassette-tape manufacturer Ampex became a sponsor of Bobby's F2 program starting with the second race of the 1979 season at Thruxton, England. Though their deal was structured as a race-by-race agreement, Ampex sponsored the car at all of the remaining events. (Michael C. Brown)

Chicago to Dave Wilson, who was then the sales manager at Chevron, to run in the works Formula Two program with Brian Hart engines."

Bobby created a limited partnership to raise the funds. Mike gave him $25,000, he borrowed $25,000 from Oliver Stahel, which he paid back with interest, and a fellow involved in the SCCA, Dave Morrell, gave him some money.

"Then I had to find the other twenty-five grand, and we started piecemealing it together," Bobby continues. "That's when I met Geoff Mulligan, the European marketing manager at Ampex [a cassette tape manufacturer]. A guy named Craig Ellsworth from Chicago actually put the deal together. To begin with, they bought one race. We didn't have anything on the car at Silverstone [England], and then I sold them on Thruxton [England]. Then we went to Europe, again race-by-race. Ampex paid me only $5,000 a race, and in those days that was almost enough for a bare-bones effort. But we were always cutting corners, and unfortunately it showed as the year went on."

The season began well enough, with a good third at Silverstone and an even stronger run in round two of the championship at Hockenheim, Germany. The race at Hockenheim was run in two heats with the final result decided on aggregate times, and after falling to the tail of the field in the first heat following a stop to change a punctured tire, Bobby finished a close third in the second heat behind Keke Rosberg and South African Rad Dougall. He also turned the race's fastest lap.

That would be Bobby's best F2 race of the year, however, as the Chevron was overshad-owed by the latest Marches and Ralts, with their more recent ground-effect aerodynamic developments. His car was also run on a shoestring budget.

"We didn't have the best equipment, but Brian Hart did his best and Chevron did their best. I got there just in time for Derek Bennett to kill himself in an airplane crash. He *was* Chevron. He

was the originator, owner and designer, and the guiding light for everyone at Chevron."

Another race where Bobby ran well was the street race in Pau, France. "I qualified well and was second or third in the race behind Teo Fabi," Bobby recalls. "There's a kink right at the start/finish line and he was chopping me every lap, and I just wouldn't give way one lap, and we went in there, and there was no way we'd both fit. That was the end of the race for both of us. It was kind of stupid on my part, really."

And of course there was the Nurburgring, the original 14-mile circuit through the Eifel mountains that Bobby raced on in F3 in 1978 and in F2 in 1979. "For every guy who bitched about safety at the Nurburgring, just as many guys reveled in how wonderful it was," Bobby says, smiling broadly. "When I raced at the old, original Nurburgring, it still just had hedgerows alongside the road."

Bobby qualified fifth for the F2 race at the Nurburgring with a time that would have put him twelfth on the grid for the F1 race the year before. He was running second in the race when his engine blew. Despite his short-lived run, the event was a gratifying experience.

"One thing I remember about the Nurburgring was there were two sections just after the Karussell that looked very similar but had very different endings," Bobby says. "One section

At the Nurburgring, Bobby lifts two wheels off the ground as he negotiates one of the 'Ring's infamous jumps. He loved the challenge of the great German road course, and the Nurburgring remains one of his favorite circuits. (LAT Photographic)

At Zandvoort, Holland, in July 1979, Bobby battled hard with the leaders but dropped out because of an oil leak. Here, he chases Derek Daly into the Tarzan curve. "Daly and I banged wheels for a while coming down into there," Bobby remarks. (LAT Photographic)

got tight, ending with a second-gear corner. The other opened up into a fifth-gear corner. I remember one time finally hitting the second exit, the faster of the two, just exactly right. The car was light, and I came up over the crest of the hill right to the edge of the road. It was one of those things where you never saw the edge, or the line, because you were right on it. When you came out of a difficult corner like that at the Nurburgring and you did it just right, it gave you a tremendous feeling of satisfaction."

In the middle of the year Bobby was hoping again to get into F1 when James Hunt decided to retire from racing. "I was on the phone to Oliver and Walter, saying, 'OK, I'm here. Where do you want me and when?'"

Added to Bobby's pressures in competing in F2 and trying to regain his spot with Wolf was the fact that his relationship with Lori was deteriorating. The strain of their living and traveling in Europe so Bobby could follow his dream while Lori had effectively put her own career on hold was starting to show.

"At the June meeting at Hockenheim [the second F2 race of the year at the track] I really drove way over my head because I just wanted to show everybody that I deserved to be in

Formula One. I think we ended up sixth overall. I didn't drive very well. I was way too aggressive. I was banging wheels, and it was just a bad deal. And, of course, my marriage was falling apart, and nobody from Wolf was returning my calls."

"I think it was because of Peter Warr, frankly," Bobby adds, "and they ended up going with Keke Rosberg. That really took me aback. I remember being very disappointed. I thought there was a relationship there and, obviously, there wasn't."

Rosberg's memory of that time reflects the tough attitude of European open-wheel racing. "It was very interesting in those days to see an American guy trying to settle into Europe," Rosberg remarks. "Bobby went the whole way and even lived in England. He did it in a very proper way, and we all respected him. That was a do-or-die time for us all.

On the streets of Pau, France, Bobby ran in the top three until he and Teo Fabi collided when the two vied for position in a spot on the track that was only large enough for one. That ended the race for them both. Here Bobby leads Italian driver Siegfried Stohr. (LAT Photographic)

"I remember meeting Bobby again many years later at a cocktail party in Miami," Rosberg adds. "I was excited to meet him again, and I was surprised when he was very cool to me. I went home and thought about it and decided it was because I beat him everywhere, so it was probably more difficult for him to have the same fond memories. At first I thought I was quite an arrogant bastard even to think like this, but then I went further and further into it, and I think that's exactly what it was.

"We did Formula Atlantic and Formula 2 and some CanAm together. I went around the world with Bobby, probably more than any other racing driver during those days. My feeling was it was great to race with Bobby. It was a great feeling because you knew he would race you hard but clean. But Bobby was married, and we had a little bit different interests in life. We didn't spend a lot of social time together."

When the offer came in midsummer to replace George Follmer in the Prophet CanAm car back in the States, Bobby's European adventure began to wane. In fact, he decided to pass up the year's last F2 race in August at Donington Park in England, preferring to drive Kaplan's car in a CanAm race at Brainerd, Minnesota, on the same day. "This aggravated the Chevron people a bit. Geoff Mulligan and the people at Ampex were more understanding, and Patrick Gaillard took my place at Donington."

Bobby made his reluctant return to the United States in July of 1979. That summer, because of a family illness, Lori had moved back and taken a job in Chicago. They began to formally separate.

Follmer had been quite competitive with the Prophet in the 1978 CanAm series, winning one race and finishing fifth in the championship. In 1979, however, Follmer took just a single fourth place from the year's opening four CanAm races. He struggled to match the pace set by Jacky Ickx in Carl Haas's Lola and the pair of Newman Racing Spyders driven by Keke Rosberg and Elliott Forbes-Robinson. Kaplan then fired Follmer.

In more action at the Nurburgring, Bobby sprints through the Karussell taking care to keep his Chevron hunkered down in the lower, banked portion of the corner. (LAT Photographic)

In his CanAm debut in the Prophet at Watkins Glen, Bobby ran in third place before retiring from the race with overheating problems. The car failed to run the distance again at Road America a few weeks later, but Bobby was third at Brainerd and second at Three Rivers before scoring his first CanAm win at Laguna Seca, California. In the final CanAm race of 1979, at Riverside, Bobby finished second to champion Jacky Ickx, and Kaplan offered him a firm deal to drive for him in 1980.

"At that point I was looking forward to doing Formula Two again the next year," Bobby says. "Geoff Mulligan tried to put something together in Europe. We almost got a deal with Ron Dennis at McLaren to run a BMW in the 1980 ProCar series, but I didn't really want to do that. I wanted to race Formula cars, you know, and Dennis wanted a lot of money, somewhere around $200,000, and in the end the CanAm thing back here in the States was just a much better deal."

Because his financial situation was so tenuous at that time, Bobby faced a difficult choice. He could put together another season in Formula Two and continue racing in Europe. Choosing his alternative, racing in the CanAm, would earn him $50,000, which he felt was good money in 1980.

"So at the end of '79, on one hand I was struggling," Bobby says. "I owed money because I had to borrow money to fulfill my commitment to Chevron. And on the other hand, I had a contract and an agreement in hand for next year, and they wanted to pay a good salary. What should I do?"

At the end of the year, after scoring his first CanAm win at Laguna Seca in October, and going through considerable soul-searching, Bobby decided to leave Europe and race full-time for Kaplan in the 1980 CanAm series. He derived immense enjoyment and satisfaction from his two years of racing in Europe, despite his struggles with limited funding and a

Opposite: Bobby gets ready for his CanAm debut driving Herb Kaplan's Prophet-Chevy at Watkins Glen. "We ran as high as third in the race, but the car overheated," Bobby says. "There were little radiators in that car, and they just couldn't cool it effectively." (Geoffrey Hewitt)

Right: In the garage at Watkins Glen during the August weekend of Bobby's first CanAm race. After the pressures of having to finance his F2 program, Bobby was delighted to be paid outright for driving Herb Kaplan's Prophet. (Geoffrey Hewitt)

At the Lumbermen's long-distance sports car race August 26, 1979, at Mid-Ohio, racer Brian Redman invited Bobby to co-drive with himself and car builder–owner Tony Cicale in Cicale's under-2-liter CanAm car. Here Bobby steers through the esses on his way to a surprising victory. (Robert Harmeyer Jr.)

failing marriage. Bobby's time in Europe didn't get him into a full-time F1 drive, but he remains deeply satisfied with his accomplishments from that period.

"I think I can say with some certainty," he says, "if you look at all the Americans who have competed in the junior categories in Europe, nobody has done as well as I did. I competed against the guys who were the leaders in Formula One for the next ten years, and I competed equally with them."

Near the end of 1979, Bobby almost stumbled into racing in the Lumbermen's 500, a special open sports car race at Mid-Ohio. That race propelled him into thinking less about racing formula cars and more about racing in IMSA's Camel GT series and the FIA's (Federation Internationale de l'Automobile) World Sports Car Championship. "I was there just to look around," Bobby recounts. "And Brian Redman offered me a ride in Tony Cicale's car, and we won the race! That was a lot of fun. In fact, it was one of my biggest paydays in quite some time."

Bobby steers through turn five during his second race in the Prophet at Road America in Elkhart Lake, Wisconsin, on July 22, 1979. Overheating problems again blunted his attack. (Dan Boyd)

Redman, an Englishman who now lives in Florida and runs a series of vintage races, is one of the most accomplished sports car drivers. He has sixteen World Championship sports car race victories to his credit, as well as twelve IMSA GT wins and the 1981 IMSA championship. Redman also won the American Formula 5000 championship three years running from 1974 through 1976. Before that, he dabbled in Formula One, driving in a dozen races for five different teams between 1968 and 1974.

"I knew Bobby a little bit, and I'd read about the result from a Formula Two race at the Nurburgring, where he ran third before his engine blew up," Redman explains. "To be able to do what he did at the Nurburgring, where he had so little experience against the Europeans, displayed exceptional talent. That drive at the Nurburgring was what really brought him to my attention.

"That weekend of the Lumbermen's, he was just there, hanging out, and it was a long race, a six-hour race, and I said to Tony Cicale, why don't we have Bobby drive as well? And he said, OK, and that's what happened.

"Brian was always supportive and helpful to me," Bobby says. "He always gave me advice, and I think he actually cared. He's one of the few guys who really understood and wanted to help—a really good guy."

By the close of 1979, it became increasingly apparent to both Bobby and Lori that their marriage would not survive two sets of dreams. Lori wanted to stay in Chicago and continue to pursue more schooling and a career, while Bobby had aspirations Lori could not reconcile. In the spring of 1980, they agreed to end their marriage. "I think our breakup affected me

Opposite: Bobby and his longtime rival, Keke Rosberg, lead the field through the esses on the pace lap at Riverside. Behind them is Geoff Lees (2), Jacky Ickx (1), and Elliott Forbes-Robinson (4). Bobby finished second to Ickx, who was that year's CanAm champion, driving for Carl Haas. (Paul Webb)

Below: A portrait of the twenty-six-year-old Bobby from late 1979. (Hal Crocker)

in '79, and my driving to an extent," Bobby says, "because you are worried about what is going on. You are upset. In '78, it wasn't that way. I was really concentrating on trying to build my career, but in '79 Lori's and my personal issues started to affect my ability to focus, or perform, or even to live.

"That was a pretty lonely period of time, especially living in England alone, and especially northern England. If I had been living in London, it might not have been so lonely, but living in Southport, Lancashire, was in many ways like being at the end of the world."

Bobby believes the divorce ultimately had a beneficial effect on his approach to life. "Lori got me back into racing, and when we got divorced, that was the thing that triggered me to mature," he says. "When I look back, I was a late bloomer as far as being businesslike about racing. I think I talked the talk, but I'm not so sure that I walked the walk. I think the divorce kind of awakened me in a number of ways. It focused me on what really was important in that, in the end, it was going to be all up to you. You had to do it. It wasn't going to happen any other way."

The final blow that year came in December when Bobby crashed an Arrows F1 car he was testing at Silverstone. The car's owner was interested in Bobby driving in the following year's British National F1 series, but the testing accident ended that possibility.

"To this day I don't know what happened," Bobby says. "It was cold and damp, typical English winter weather, but everything was fine. I don't remember much about it, but I went off and one of the fence poles hit me in the head. It hit so hard it turned my helmet sideways. I guess they found me and I was trying to swallow my tongue and I was half out of the car, apparently.

"The only thing I remember is coming to and the track manager, 'Silverstone Sid,' was there. Sid had a voice that was recognizable, and as we were in the ambulance heading toward the hospital, he was talking to me. He said, 'Do you know who you are? Do you know who I am?' If it had been any other voice, I probably wouldn't have known, but even through the fog I could figure out exactly where I was."

Bobby spent three days in the hospital in England, just before Christmas in 1979. He had wrecked the Arrows, but he never saw it again to assess the damage himself. "It was a lousy end of the year. I went to my grandmother's in Largo, Florida, for Christmas, and I think I was still spacey from the accident. When I took change out of my pocket, I didn't just look at it and know that was seventy-five cents. I had to add it up. I was spaced out for three weeks."

"I wanted to race as many types of cars as possible."

After the misery Bobby went through at the end of 1979, things looked good for 1980. He had agreed to drive again in the CanAm series for Herb Kaplan, who assured Bobby he was going to retire the venerable Prophet and buy a new Lola. The Prophet was based on a four-year-old Lola Formula 5000 chassis, while the new Lola T530 was the first car designed specifically for the new CanAm formula rather than being a rehashed F5000 car. It was extremely likely, therefore, that the new Lola would be the thing to have in 1980.

Bobby was also able to sell Ampex, through Geoff Mulligan, on sponsoring Kaplan's car. The sponsorship began on an experimental basis at the end of 1979 with the Prophet turned out in black with striking red and yellow stripes. It looked good, and Bobby was justifiably excited about the new year, back in the USA.

Almost from the start, however, there were hints that maybe Bobby hadn't made the right move. First, Barry Green, the new manager of Paul Newman's Budweiser CanAm team, called to offer him a ride in one of Newman's new March CanAm cars. Bobby told Green that he had made a verbal commitment to Kaplan and reluctantly couldn't accept his

Above: German veteran Jurgen Barth joined Bobby and Garretson in the Watkins Glen 6 Hours. "Lancia and other European manufacturers had sent cars over to compete," Bobby says. "I qualified on the pole, then in the race, the engine blew up on about the fourth lap. It was unbelievable." (Robert Harmeyer Jr.)

Opposite: Drastic measures were called for to make the aging Prophet competitive with the new Lolas. Kaplan's small team tried to improve the car aerodynamically by covering the rear wheels and attempting to redirect the airflow through and underneath the chassis. (Geoffrey Hewitt)

In 1980 Bobby met Debi Kuhl at the Mosport CanAm race, and they were married five months later. Here they relax near Debi's cottage located on the Canadian coastline. (Rahal Collection)

The Prophet looked good in its season-long Ampex livery, but by 1980 the car was outdated by Lola's new T530 chassis, and Bobby found himself struggling to keep up. The year turned out to be disastrous. (Hal Crocker)

extremely tempting offer. A little later, Carl Haas also called to offer his car to Rahal, but again Bobby felt he had to turn it down.

"I'd given my word to Herb Kaplan, who'd given me my chance in the Prophet, and I told him I would drive for him again the following year. He wanted to pay me $50,000, which was a lot of money in those days."

If the late approaches from Green and Haas hadn't created enough second-guessing in Bobby's mind, one can imagine what he thought when Kaplan informed him that he wasn't buying a new Lola after all. The Prophet, Kaplan insisted, was going to continue in business for another year.

In 1979 the Prophet had served Bobby well. He scored his first CanAm victory at Laguna Seca and battled with the spectacular Keke Rosberg, whom Bobby had raced against regularly in Formula Atlantic and F2. The six CanAm races he drove in 1979 further enhanced his already strong domestic reputation and added to his hopes for what 1980 might bring. "Rosberg and I were on the front row in almost every race," Bobby recalls, "although Jackie Ickx won the championship with consistent finishes in Carl Haas's car."

Bobby had been first or second in the last three CanAm races of 1979, but by the following year, the Prophet was out-of-date. After finishing third in the 1980 season opener, Bobby didn't make the podium again until finishing third in the seventh and eighth rounds of the championship at Three Rivers and Road Atlanta in September. Bobby was a distant fifth in the championship and could only look with envy at Patrick Tambay's championship-winning record of six victories, including the year's first four races, aboard Carl Haas's Lola T530.

"In 1979, I was a hot commodity," Bobby says, shaking his head, "but at the end of 1980 nobody wanted to have anything to do with me. You make the wrong change or wrong deal, and the car is a dog, and at the end of the year, nobody's calling you. It can be pretty amazing, but that's what happened to me that year.

"What was particularly embarrassing about 1980 was that I'd convinced Davey Evans and Tony Connor, who had been Carl Haas's main guys, to join me. What looked so good on paper turned out to be such a disaster."

The best thing that happened to Bobby that year was that he met Debi Kuhl. "The first time I met Debi was the Mosport CanAm in June of 1980," Bobby recalls. "I had just come back from Le Mans. Debi had met a fellow from Ampex and was dating him. Lori and I were in the midst of our divorce, and Debi and I kind of hit it off. I don't know if it was love at first sight, but there were definitely some fireworks."

Debi grew up in Northport, New York, on Long Island, and was working for Aer Lingus at John F. Kennedy airport when she met Bobby. "I had no interest in racing and had never been to a race," Debi says. "I met Bobby there, and a couple of weeks later he invited me to

Chicago, and we just had a wonderful time. He was very much the gentleman, as usual, and within five months we were married.

"Bobby is very worldly. He's very knowledgeable. No matter where you are, he knows something about the history of the people, or something about the landscape, and that really attracted me to him, that he could be in any situation and talk to anyone about anything. Bobby was very different from what is supposed to be your typical race car driver. I guess in my mind I always thought I'd marry a rancher or something because I always loved animals and just never considered my life being the way it is now."

During this time, the CanAm was faltering under the SCCA's weak leadership while IMSA's Camel GT series was beginning to flourish. IMSA had a series sponsor, which the CanAm lacked, and was adding races to its schedule as the CanAm series was contracting. While struggling with the Prophet in the 1980 CanAm series, Bobby branched out into IMSA and World Championship GT racing, including making his first start in the Le Mans 24 Hours. Bobby co-drove Bob Garretson's Porsche 935 in six long-distance sports car races that year, his best result coming in a 1,000 kilometer FIA World Sports Car round at Mosport, where he finished third, co-driving with Ted Field and Danny Ongais.

"I started to look at sports cars—IMSA and the World Sports Car Championship—because I wanted to do more racing," Bobby says. "I wanted to race as many types of cars as possible, and it really worked out because, in the end, after my lousy 1980 CanAm season, sports car racing kept me going until I took over the Budweiser CanAm car in the middle of '81."

The 1980 CanAm season opened at Sears Point, or Golden State Raceway, as it was then called, in Northern California. Bobby finished third, but the Prophet was already getting trounced by the new Lolas. Here he leads Dick Guider's Ralt through a turn. (Marc Sproule)

Preparation expert Garretson ran Dick Barbour's IMSA team and drove one of the cars, sponsored by Apple Computers. John Fitzpatrick drove the other 935, sponsored by Sachs, and won eight races and the IMSA championship in 1980. Garretson says Bobby learned some valuable race craft during his time with the team.

"Even though he was a very good driver, I think he needed a little maturity," Garretson says, "and I think I was able to provide that for him and teach him that there are a lot of factors involved in winning a race. You've got to do all the preparation, you've got to run the race right, and you've got to be lucky. You've got to be there at the finish before you can win the race. Bobby had a difficult time not wanting to go out and thrash right from the very beginning. But as time went on he got better and better at that part."

Barbour and Garretson split during the winter. Garretson planned to run his own team in 1981 with Bobby driving for him for prize money. Then Ralph Kent-Cooke and Roy Woods asked Garretson to manage their team, which was going to race a new Lola T600 for Brian Redman when the car was ready in April. Garretson agreed to merge his operation with Cooke-Woods, and Redman teamed with Garretson and Bobby in Garretson's 935 for the early-season long-distance races.

Bobby drove the 1981 Daytona 24 Hours with Bob Garretson and Brian Redman in Garretson's Porsche 935. "Brian asked where we were placed when I turned the car over to him late in the night," Bobby says. "When I told him we were leading, he got mad! He thought I'd chased down the faster guys. I said 'Brian, I didn't do anything, they're all falling out!'" (Robert Harmeyer Jr.)

The trio started the season in the best way, winning the Daytona 24 Hours. They started about fifteenth and took the lead fairly early. "I was going around saying, 'Too soon! Too soon!' " Redman recalls, because he was concerned they would overtax the car early in the race. "But the only problem we had was a broken exhaust header, which Greg Eliff, the Garretson mechanic, changed in about 15 minutes, laying under the car with all this red hot metal over him, shouting for wrenches. It was a great run, and Bobby did a perfect job."

"You told him what you wanted, and it was done," Garretson says of Bobby's endurance-driving skills. "If you told him to speed up, he sped up. If you wanted him to slow down, he slowed down. You never had to worry about the car getting damaged or anything like that."

Bobby and Garretson continued through the next four IMSA races, but growing arguments between Garretson and partners Cooke and Woods created a rift between them. Bobby was supposed to drive a new Lola T600 GTP car for Cooke-Woods that year. The Lola was a purpose-built, ground-effect car that clearly outperformed the production-based Porsche 935s.

Bobby recalls the intrigue surrounding the short-lived Cooke-Woods team and how Debi had sensed that all was not right between Bobby and the team. "Brian was going to retire, and I was going to take his place, and they were going to announce it after the race.

I'll never forget, we went to a restaurant and Debi said, 'Something's wrong. There's something wrong here.' And I said, 'No, no.' And she kept saying, 'Something's wrong.' And sure enough, there was. She called it. I was on the street, game over. Garretson had had it up to here with

At Road Atlanta, Bobby applies some opposite lock as he slides the car through a turn. "We tried to make the Prophet a ground-effect car à la the Frissbee, which was the same concept," Bobby says. "Davey Evans and Tony Connor did that conversion, but the car was a dog." (Hal Crocker)

Ralph Kent-Cooke, so we were both out of there. They pulled the plug on my car after Laguna Seca at the beginning of May."

Debi recalls her memory of that dinner. "I became very tense for some reason. I don't know why, because I'm not at all a psychic person. Bobby was sitting to the left of me and I kept having this awful feeling. I said, 'Bobby, don't do this. It's not going to work. Somebody's pulling a scam here.'"

With only six weeks to prepare, Cooke and Woods decided they would enter a Lola-Porsche at Le Mans for Bobby and Redman. Redman was adamantly against it, and the hasty effort was a complete failure. A drive shaft broke on the first lap, and turbocharger problems robbed the engine of power. Neither Bobby nor Redman was able to complete any flying laps in the car during practice, and they failed to qualify for the race. "I remember Bobby saying, 'Let me try; I'll qualify it.' But it just wouldn't go," Redman says. "Ralph Cooke got the whole team together on Monday morning at breakfast and fired everybody except for John Bright and myself. We had a race the following weekend at Mid-Ohio with the Chevy-powered Lola, and we got a new crew together, new truck drivers, everything."

Bobby finished the year scrounging rides wherever he could. "I was in a lot of different cars that year. It was one of those deals where I was just desperate to drive anything." He drove one of Bob Akin's 935s in two European long-distance races. Co-driving with Akin and Peter Lovett, he was sixth in May's Silverstone 6 Hours, then went to the Nurburgring for the 1000 Kilometers, but the German classic ended in catastrophe, with Bobby involved.

Below: Co-driving with Bob Garretson in his Porsche 935, Bobby finished a conservative second in the Brands Hatch 1000K. For Garretson, that placing cinched his FIA World Endurance title and allowed Bobby to finish third in the same championship. (LAT Photographic)

Below right: Bobby douses himself with water immediately after the finish of the Glen Six Hours. (Hal Crocker)

Bobby tangled with Guy Edwards's car in a tight corner just before the Karussell, and after both of them scrambled uninjured from their ruined cars, Herbert Muller crashed his Porsche 908 into the wreckage, creating a massive conflagration. Muller was burned to death in the ensuing fire, and the race was stopped. "That was not a good day," Bobby reflects. "It was bad, very bad."

Bobby stayed in IMSA's championship hunt for most of the summer, jumping from car to car. After taking fifth with Gianpiero Moretti at Elkhart Lake at the end of August, Bobby was still second in points to Redman, although he faded in the end to fourth in the championship, as he missed two of the year's last three IMSA races.

"The long races, I was with Moretti in the 'Moby Dick' car, which was a unique car," Bobby says. "It was purpose-built from the ground up. It was an ex-factory car with right-hand drive and left-hand shift, whereas all the production 935s were left-hand drive, and they were all built on 911 frames. [Reinhold] Joest actually took care of the car, and it always had strong motors. That thing was faster than hell."

Bobby rejoined Bob Garretson for the year's final FIA sports car race at Brands Hatch in September and the IMSA finale at Daytona at the end of November. They finished second in the 1000K race at Brands Hatch, ensuring veteran Garretson of that year's FIA World Endurance Driver's Championship and helping Bobby to third in the same championship. "We played it conservatively," Garretson says. "We just did as well as we had to. To win the championship meant everything to me."

A month earlier, Bobby had come close to winning the free-for-all Lumbermen's race at Mid-Ohio for the second year in a row, co-driving this time with good friend Jim Trueman in Trueman's Ralt-Hart 2-liter CanAm car.

"Anything with wheels and fenders on it could run in that race, basically," Bobby comments. "A Frissbee CanAm car qualified on the pole, and we qualified second in our 2-liter CanAm car. Jim and I should have won. We were leading, but Jim had gotten hit early in the race by a Corvette, and with about ten laps to go, the left front suspension started falling off the car while I was driving." Bobby dropped from the lead to fifth at the checkered flag as his crash-damaged car fell apart.

The big turn for Bobby that year came in early September, when he was invited by team manager Barry Green to replace Al Unser Sr. in one of Paul Newman's March CanAm cars. Green had known Bobby since Bobby's Formula Atlantic days, when Green was a mechanic for Fred Opert's Atlantic team. After spinning wrenches for a few years for Opert, Green returned to his native Australia to race Formula Fords, then went to England, where he raced a Formula Three Chevron in 1979, and reacquainted himself with Bobby, who raced the F2 Chevron that year. When Green crashed and broke a leg in an F3 race, Bobby's younger brother took care of him for a few days.

"In 1981, we were running Teo Fabi and Al Sr.," Green says, "and Al didn't like the car at all and decided to go his own way. We were looking for a hired gun, someone that would

Bobby drove one of Paul Newman's March CanAm cars in the second half of the 1981 season, replacing Al Unser Sr. Here he approaches turn eleven at Laguna Seca just before a spark plug wire shorted out. After that, the engine fired on only seven of eight cylinders, and Bobby fell to ninth place. (Marc Sproule)

come in and help Teo win the championship. Bobby had to run second in a lot of cases, but he did a tremendous job for us and really rekindled the team. It was a fun four races we did together. The best one was at Mosport, where Teo had just had his appendix out on the Tuesday before the race, and we qualified one-two and raced one-two the whole race. Bobby had to sit behind Teo. He was a lot faster than Teo at the time."

"Remember," Bobby notes, "this was the team I had a chance to drive for in 1980, but I said no because I had made a commitment to Herb Kaplan. Then in '81 they hired Fabi and Al Sr., and Fabi kept smoking Al Sr. So I started at Mosport and qualified on pole ahead of Fabi, and I led the first ten laps, and then, right in front of the pits, I just backed off so everybody could see that I was letting him pass. It was Fabi and me, just like the old McLaren CanAm days. It was just the two of us the whole race."

In the remaining three races, however, Bobby was entirely out of luck, although he did finish fourth in the last CanAm race of the season at Las Vegas. "We had some very good races, and some that weren't so good," he remarks. Teammate Fabi scored four wins that year, more than anyone else, but it wasn't enough to beat Geoff Brabham's consistency in Team VDS's neat VDS 001. Designed by Tony Cicale, who had built the U2L car Bobby had shared with Redman and Cicale to win the 1979 Lumbermen's race, the VDS 001 was based on a Lola T530 chassis and driven to good effect by Brabham, who won just two races but took the championship with a stronger overall finishing record than Fabi.

Team VDS was owned by Belgian Count Rudi van der Straten, and the team raced in the United States from 1976 through 1983, first in Formula 5000, then in the CanAm, and finally in Indy cars. When VDS won the CanAm championship with Brabham in 1981, the team was run by Steve Horne, a New Zealand–raised Englishman. Horne had come to the United States with Team VDS in 1976 and had quickly impressed people with his ability to get things done. So it wasn't surprising that as the 1981 season wound down, Horne was heading toward a fateful new relationship with Bobby and Jim Trueman with the creation of Truesports.

"In '81 it seemed my career was more likely ending than continuing," Bobby says. "The only thing that really kept me going by midsummer was the fact that Jim wanted to go Indy car racing and wanted me to drive for him in '82." However, there was competition for the seat from Australian driver Vern Schuppan, who had finished third in the 1981 Indianapolis 500. "I remember Jim said there were going to be certain demands he was going to put on me, and if I was smart I'd accept them. He wanted me to help set up Truesports, find sponsorship money, and basically, he didn't want me driving anything else for any other team unless I got his approval. I said, 'Sure, whatever you say.' It was the best offer I had, by far."

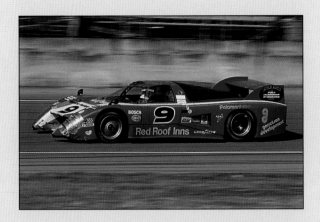

"That was the genesis of Truesports."

Bobby traces the creation of Truesports to the 1981 Indy 500, when Vern Schuppan finished third behind Bobby Unser and Mario Andretti driving a three-year-old McLaren-Cosworth run by Herb and Rose Wysard's little team. Jim Trueman's Red Roof Inns motel chain was the primary sponsor of Schuppan's car that day, which inspired Trueman to start his own Indy car team. Ever the confident optimist, Trueman figured that if the Wysards could put together an operation that could finish third at the Speedway, then a little application from talented, motivated fellows like Bobby and him would get them to Victory Lane.

Bobby and Trueman had known each other from Bobby's early racing days. They were SCCA club racing buddies, competing in the Chicago and MidWest regions. Trueman lived in Columbus, Ohio, and was busily building the Red Roof chain. His business plan was to provide simple, inexpensive rooms at locations immediately off any interstate, and the chain grew steadily, expanding across the Midwest and Northeast. Trueman liked Bobby, recognizing from the start that he was a pretty talented driver, and he had given him a few

Above: Bobby qualified the March GTP car on the pole at Daytona, but Trueman and he encountered a long series of mechanical problems during the race. They didn't make the finish. (Hal Crocker)

Opposite: While longtime friends Bobby and Jim Trueman created the Truesports CART team, they also drove together in a series of early-season IMSA races in 1982. Here Bobby prepares the March-Chevy GTP car before the Daytona 24 Hours. Note the demisting filaments in the windshield. (Rahal collection)

Truesports made its CART debut at Phoenix in 1982. Steve Horne gives Bobby "rabbit ears" as team owner Jim Trueman sticks out his tongue. Despite the lighthearted start, their race was a complete disaster. (Christine Horne)

dollars of sponsorship in exchange for Red Roof Inns stickers on most of Bobby's Formula Atlantic cars and B/Sports racers.

As the Red Roof chain grew, so did Trueman's interest in trying to race more seriously. Around this time he also decided he was going to buy and redevelop the Mid-Ohio road course, paying local farmer and track founder Les Greibling $2 million for the track, and putting more money into making Mid-Ohio one of the greenest, most agreeable road circuits in the country. And after Schuppan's third place at Indianapolis in Red Roof colors in May of 1981, Trueman told Bobby he would pay the operating expenses and hire the necessary people if Bobby could find somebody to buy the cars and engines.

"I was pleased, because it's a lot easier to find people to buy the engines, to buy something they can touch and feel, rather than just going out and finding the operating capital, which is the expensive part," Bobby says. "So I said OK, and Jim and I put together the team. That was the genesis of Truesports."

"It was the best offer I had because it was the only offer I had," Bobby adds. "I had an offer to drive the Budweiser CanAm car in '82, but the CanAm was dying. Everybody was starting to pull out, and CART was becoming the way to go."

Bobby located the space for the race shop and did a lot of the "grunt work," in his words, of setting up the new team. Then he went about finding investors among his racing friends. He was able to sell Dick Leppla, a longtime amateur and historic racer who owns the Crane and Shovel Company in Cleveland, on the idea of buying two new March Indy cars. "They

Engine builder Franz Weis (center) jokes with Paul Newman and Trueman at Las Vegas. The three knew one another from their CanAm days: Newman had run his own team; Weis built engines for top teams, including VDS; and Trueman had occasionally competed in the under-2-liter class. (Christine Horne)

were only $80,000 or $90,000 each at the time," Bobby says, "but it was a lot of money, and Dick ended up buying both."

The team bought five new turbo Cosworth DFX engines. "We must've split shares up into tenths or something," Bobby says. Mike bought one engine, while Bob Donner and Paul Pappalardo, both retired racers, bought two other engines, and a collection of amateur IMSA racers bought the last two. Other people paid for the capital equipment, and Trueman then leased the cars and engines.

The team paid the investors 10 percent of the prize money they won during the season. Each investor's share was determined proportionately by the amount of his original investment. "Those guys thought it was the best investment they'd made because we were returning 10 percent of their money," Bobby remarks. "At the end of the deal, they got the engine back. We sold the engine for them, and they split up the proceeds. So it was really a pretty good deal for everybody. For us because we didn't have capital tied up in engines, and for them because there were some tax implications and an opportunity to make back a little money and go to the races."

The big question was who would run the team. Bobby and Trueman talked to English veteran Derek Mower, who had run Bob Fletcher's race-winning United States Automobile Club (USAC) and CART team. They also talked to Australian Peter Collins, who would end up running the Lotus F1 team in the early 1990s.

"But Jim said he wanted to talk to Steve Horne," Bobby recalls. "Both of us knew Steve through the CanAm. He wasn't the friendliest guy, but he seemed to know how to get the job done, and there was a rumor he was going to leave VDS."

Horne had watched Bobby race for a number of years in Formula Atlantic and CanAm cars. "I first met Bobby, I think it was 1977 in the Tasman series," recalls Horne. "He was driving an Atlantic car for Fred Opert with Keke Rosberg. I was down there in New Zealand on my holiday helping Steve Millen with his Atlantic program, and realized then that he was going to be pretty good.

"I watched him when he drove for Herb Kaplan in the CanAm, and Bobby drove the shit out of that thing. I remember at Mosport once he stuck it in the wall, right up on the grass bank coming onto the pit straight. I think at times he overdrove it, but he was a pretty good competitor."

Horne had also gotten to know Trueman because Trueman had run a 2-liter CanAm car, and they had both served on an SCCA advisory board that was going to reinvent the CanAm into a flourishing series.

At Sebring, Bobby again qualified the March GTP car on the pole. He had sold Michelob on sponsoring the car and Bob Garretson's operation ran it, with Mauricio de Narvaez joining Bobby and Trueman as the third co-driver. Here Bobby makes a pit stop on the way to second place. (Hal Crocker)

"I decided partway through 1981 that I was going to leave VDS," Horne says. "VDS had decided to move to Texas from southern California. I went to Midland and decided I didn't want to go to Midland, so I gave VDS six months notice that I wasn't going to stay with them, and that got out around the paddock a little bit. One day, just before the last race, Trueman came to me and said, 'Would you be interested in going CART Indy car racing with me?' "

At the time, Horne told Trueman no, that he wanted to go back to England and see what his options were and take a bit of a break. Trueman and Bobby persisted, and when Horne returned from England, he met with them.

After racing with Franz Weis–built Chevrolet engines at Daytona and Sebring, the team's reduced finances dictated a switch to another supplier for Riverside and the remaining GTP races in 1982. "The car looked good," Bobby says, "but it was slower than molasses. The engines weren't worth a damn." (Bob Tronolone)

"Trueman laid it all out, and I got to know him and his businesses a little bit more, and we sat down with Bobby in Columbus and really decided to give it a shot because I felt that Trueman was ready to do it properly. He didn't have a lot of financial resources but he was pretty committed, and I felt that Bobby was a pretty good driver who had the ability to get to the next level. So we started from ground zero."

Bobby and Debi lived in an apartment in Chicago for a year before moving in November of 1981 into a small condominium in Dublin, close to the Truesports shop in Hilliard, just off Interstate 270 in the western suburbs of Columbus. Truesports started as a five-man team, with Horne in charge and Rahal's personal chief mechanic, Jim Prescott, leading the

Truesports's first race shop was located on Parkway Lane in Hilliard, Ohio. It was so small that they stored cars outside in trailers to give themselves room to work when they ran a Super Vee team in 1983. Ian Algie and Steve Horne are in this January 1982 photo. (Christine Horne)

This photo, taken in 1983, shows the cramped workspace in the Truesports raceshop. Steve Horne is at the center wearing the vest. Jimmy Prescott is on crutches, the result of a late-season accident in the pits. (Christine Horne)

small crew of mechanics. Group 44 Jaguar GTP designer Lee Dykstra was hired to work on a part-time, weekend basis as the team's engineer.

"I set up the team," Horne notes. "I employed Ian Algie, who worked for me at VDS. Bobby introduced me to Jimmy Prescott, who was an absolute diamond in the rough. The guy turned out to be brilliant. He was obviously dedicated, and still is, to Bobby. He's a great mechanic, a good guy who works hard, and he wanted to win."

Prescott was a friend of the Rahal family who had gone to high school with Bobby's brother Ian. A bricklayer by trade, Prescott worked as a mechanic on Bobby's Prophet CanAm cars in the summers of 1979 and 1980 and was back working for his brother's bricklaying business when Bobby called him just before Christmas of 1981. Bobby convinced Prescott to move to Columbus and join Truesports as Bobby's chief mechanic, a job he would retain, save for one year, through the balance of Bobby's career.

Horne describes the remainder of the recruitment drive for Truesports. "Clay Filson had worked on Jim Trueman's 2-liter program and actually at the time was working at Jim's house, looking after the horses. I remember he came in one day and we said, 'Clay, you smell funny.' And he said he'd just been mucking out the barn! We had an English guy named David Heap who came over from Williams to run the truck, and of course Spike, who was the team comedian. We had six or seven people in the beginning, and my wife, Christine, did all the books."

The small team's engines were farmed out for service and rebuilds to Franz Weis's VDS Engines operation in Midland, Texas. Former Chaparral engine man Weis had built Team VDS's CanAm engines, and Bobby, Trueman, and Horne were unanimous that Franz was the only man for the job.

Before the 1982 Indy car season began, Trueman and Bobby drove Trueman's March-Chevy GTP car in the Daytona 24 Hours and Sebring 12 Hours. The car was run by Bob Garretson with some sponsorship Bobby attracted from Anheuser-Busch brand Michelob. Bobby qualified the car on the pole at both Daytona and Sebring.

"We took the lap record in Daytona and were actually running pretty good," Bobby recounts. "I think we were running fourth, and finally, with about three hours to go, the gearbox just gave up the ghost." At Sebring, Bobby, Trueman, and Mauricio

DeNarvaez had the same problems. "We only had first and third gears, but we still finished second. We almost beat John Paul Jr. and Sr."

Horne did not approve of the IMSA program. "That was totally out of my realm," Horne grunts. "Jim asked me if I wanted to run it, and I said absolutely no way, because we had enough on our plate and I felt it would have got in the way."

Bobby also drove an F2-type car in a Codasur race at Buenos Aires, Argentina, at the beginning of that year, finishing third. "Bill France Sr. called me and said the ACCUS

[Automobile Competition Committee for the United States] wanted me to go down to Argentina for something called the Alliance for Progress to do a race in the South American F2 series. They had four-cylinder Chrysler engines and Berta chassis. It was fun."

Meanwhile, Horne and his team were thrashing to get everything organized for their collective rookie CART season. Penske Racing and Jim Hall's Chaparral team dominated Indy car racing at the time. Penske's team had won the 1979 and 1981 CART titles with Rick Mears, and Johnny Rutherford took the 1980 championship with Chaparral. During those three years, the Penske and Hall teams won twenty-nine of thirty-seven races.

The opening CART race was at Phoenix in March, and Bobby and the team went to the race without much testing. "We had run the car on the skid pad at TRC, and we'd done one road course test, I think. It was very minimal," Horne recalls.

It was a dispiriting start. Bobby qualified fifteenth, fully 2 seconds away from Rick Mears's pole lap. Everyone on the team had to learn basic oval racing techniques such as setting up the chassis with "tilt," which consists of different right and left side ride heights aimed at generating the proper weight transfer, turning moment, and traction in the corners.

"We went to Phoenix, and we were all just totally lost," Horne says, shaking his head. "Bobby was lost on the track, and we were lost on the setup. I remember Kirk Russell [CART's technical director] tried to help us a little bit. He asked how much tilt we were running, and we asked him what tilt was!"

Nor did they have the proper "skirt" arrangement. Skirts sealed the gap between the lower edges of the car's sidepods and the track surface to generate greater downforce from CART's increasingly restrictive aerodynamic rules. "Phoenix was a total disaster for us," Bobby comments. "Everybody was running skirts, and we didn't have skirts. The race wasn't going too bad, but the thing caught fire in the first pit stop." Bobby's driving suit was burning as he bailed out, and he was thankful to the nearby Penske mechanics, who threw a couple of buckets of water on him.

"I guess I went there thinking, 'No sweat. I'll run up front right away,'" Bobby says. "But when I actually got out there and started running, boy, talk about a new ball game. It was as if I'd hardly driven anything. I thought, 'Christ! This is going to be a long season.'"

Phoenix was a real eye-opener. Bobby and the brand-new team had plenty to learn about their 1982 March-Cosworth. They discovered how little they knew about Indy car racing in general and setting up a car for oval racing in particular. (Rich Chenet)

As he made his Indy car debut at Phoenix, Bobby tipped his cap to the crowd. He was thrilled to be facing a new challenge with Trueman's backing. Only a few months earlier he had feared that his racing career had come to an end. (Rich Chenet)

In addition to car setup and team organization lessons, Bobby had plenty to learn about driving and racing on ovals, something he'd never done. "Coming to grips with the ovals took a little doing," he admits. "Road racing is always a compromise. You're never going to get the car absolutely right for every corner, but on an oval, you've got to get the car handling perfectly. If not, you're nowhere.

"You can't overdrive or make up for a car's handling deficiencies on an oval. You've got to figure out how to make the car right, and you have to work more thoroughly with the team than I'd been used to doing in road racing. There was a lot to learn, and we had to learn it fast."

The team skipped the next round on the high-banked 1.5-mile Atlanta oval. Bobby drove the GTP car in the Road Atlanta, Riverside, and Laguna Seca IMSA races in April and May, while Horne and his little group worked to get ready for the month of May at Indianapolis.

Truesports was a classic group of Indy rookies, but the team gave a pretty good account of itself, as Bobby qualified seventeenth and was running a good fifth when his engine blew with only twenty-six laps—just over 60 miles—to go.

After bailing out of his burning car in the race at Phoenix, Bobby (with his back to the camera) regains his composure. Seconds before, a Penske crewman had doused Bobby's flames with a bucket of water. Roger Penske is among those who help push the Truesports car out of the pit lane. (Rich Chenet)

At Milwaukee two weeks later, Bobby was getting the feel for oval racing and was fifth fastest in practice, although an engine failure meant he qualified twenty-first. He passed five cars on the opening lap, however, and quickly moved up to seventh place before his car's suspension collapsed after only thirty-six laps.

Horne recounts the team's progress: "We'd done a few little tweaks to the car, and we had Lee Dykstra as a weekend warrior. All of us had known Lee from the CanAm, and he was magic. At Milwaukee, suddenly we were running really good. We were fourth or fifth in practice. We had a motor problem that put us behind, but at Milwaukee we suddenly started to get competitive and get the hang of what was going on. And it just went up-wards from there."

The Le Mans 24 Hours was the following weekend, in the middle of June, and the event brought an end to that year's sports car racing for Bobby and Trueman. "That was a complete fiasco," Bobby says disgustedly. "I had gotten Michelob to sponsor the car, but a guy named Brooks Frybarger ran the operation. He didn't have any money, and the engine was no good. It was way down on power, and the car was slow down the straight. It had too much drag as well."

The car arrived late for practice, and Bobby qualified in the midfield. "It was just one disaster after another," Bobby says. "We ran three hours in the race, and finally the fuel tank split and there was gas everywhere. Like I say, it was a disaster, so we just went home. That was the end of our March sports car program in '82. It was a classic case of 'If you can't do it right, don't do it all.'"

After the car broke, Bobby, Trueman, and friends drove to Paris before flying home. "We went to Paris, and I took everybody to lunch at a place in the Champs Elysées called Fouquets," Bobby tells the story. "There was Debi and me, Jim, and a bunch of friends, and about 70 percent of the party had steak tartar, and the next day they were sicker than dogs, including yours truly.

"The next morning everybody was white, and you could hear the poor wretches in the hotel room next door. I have a cast-iron stomach, and it was everything I could do to keep from throwing up. Luckily, I didn't have to fly home that day, but Jim and everybody who had the steak tartar spent the entire flight back in the john."

Two weeks later, the inaugural CART race took place at Cleveland's Burke Lakefront Airport. It was the first road course of the season and was run over 500 kilometers in fearsome 99-degree heat and 90 percent humidity. Bobby qualified second and drove a smart race, pacing himself in the early stages, then coming on strong toward the end. He ran fourth or fifth for much of the race, survived a midrace tangle with Al Unser while trying to pass Unser, then led the race's final twenty-five laps after passing Mario Andretti and Rick

Above: Bobby tries vainly to wring competitive speed from the GTP car at Le Mans and qualifies in the midfield. Trueman didn't even get a chance to qualify because the car was so unreliable. After a host of problems, a split fuel tank three hours into the race was the final blow to their attempt. (Robert Harmeyer Jr.)

Opposite: Bobby belts himself into the GTP car at Le Mans. By this time, their GTP program was in serious disarray. The operation was underfinanced, and the lack of horsepower and the car's slipshod preparation at the long, fast track meant it was entirely noncompetitive. (Rich Chenet)

Right: Trueman and Bobby pose together in the pits at Le Mans prior to the start of the race. Their adventure at La Sarthe would not last much longer. The man on the left is unidentified. (Rahal collection)

Below: In victory lane at Cleveland, Bobby triumphantly raises his first Indy car winner's trophy to the sky. He had driven a canny race in hot, humid conditions that seemed to tax the cars as heavily as they did the drivers. (Robert Harmeyer Jr.)

Mears in quick succession. He beat Andretti by 19 seconds in one of the toughest races of his life. "I took it easy in the early going," Bobby explained after the race. "I wanted to save the tires and the car. I didn't want to abuse anything. It was a very hard race. Over the last fifteen or twenty laps, my head was falling off," he said, referring to the exertion of his neck muscles in withstanding the high cornering forces.

It was only Bobby's fourth Indy car start, and he was the first rookie to win a USAC or CART race in twelve years. Right there on the shore of Lake Erie, only 20 miles from his birthplace in Medina and 100 miles north of his adopted home, Bobby turned himself and Truesports into Ohio heroes.

"We surprised everybody," Horne says with a smile. "I don't think we surprised ourselves. We felt like we were making progress, and we felt that because Cleveland was a road course, we'd have a shot, and we won—500Ks, there in all that heat and humidity, was really hard work!"

For Bobby, the Cleveland victory was all-important. "That race really put us on the map," he says. "Six or eight months earlier I'd been calling Roger [Penske] and Pat [Patrick] looking for a ride, and it was, 'Don't call us, we'll call you.' And probably within two months of that race, they were calling me, especially Pat."

With his first Indy car win under his belt, Bobby's confidence reached new heights, and he was a contender to win in most of the remaining races that year. He drove another strong race to finish third in the Michigan 500 behind Patrick teammates Gordon Johncock and Andretti, and ahead of Al Unser. Bobby qualified fourth and really impressed in August's Milwaukee 200, beating Andretti for second behind Tom Sneva. By then Bobby was up to third in points, and had already wrapped up rookie of the year. For once, momentum was on his side.

In the Pocono 500, Bobby finished third behind Penske teammates Mears and Kevin Cogan, and at Riverside for another 500-kilometer road race, he qualified third and was running second to Cogan when a driveshaft joint broke about a third of the way into the race. At Elkhart Lake, one of his favorite tracks, Bobby qualified second and took command of the race. He was leading with five laps to go when rain started to fall. Thinking the race would be red-flagged, Bobby and Horne gambled on staying out, rather than pitting for fuel.

"It was very slick out there," Bobby said at the time, "and the starter had the red flag in his hand. We were afraid we might get caught in the pits when the red

flag came out, but instead we ran out of fuel." He wound up finishing third after being towed to the pits and refueling.

Then in September, Bobby scored his first oval track victory, winning the Michigan 150 by outdueling Mario Andretti, helped by a rapid final pit stop that got Bobby out ahead of Andretti. "I remember Jim calling up after the race and asking how we did, because he was running a CanAm race that day," Steve Horne recalls. "I said, 'We won,' and he absolutely refused to believe it. Somebody else had to get on the phone to tell him."

Bobby qualified fourth and finished two laps down in fifth place at the Phoenix season closer behind Sneva, Mears, Andretti, and Cogan. He wasn't very happy with his car's handling that weekend but finished second in the championship to Mears, ahead of Andretti, Johncock, and Sneva. "As the season progressed," Horne says, "we all learned a lot about Indy car racing, and Bobby, I think, rose to another level. I think that level was always there, but we gave him the platform to do it on."

Bobby was the runaway winner of CART's rookie of the year award and had finally established himself as a front-line racing driver. He had an offer from Pat Patrick for the next season to replace Andretti, who had decided to leave Patrick and join the new Newman-Haas CART team for 1983.

"I visited Pat's shop in Indianapolis at the end of '82," Bobby says, "and I remember thinking, 'Man, this is the big time.' Patrick Racing, you know. But I just felt such a huge sense of obligation to Jim that I couldn't leave him."

At the end of the year, he and Debi moved into their first house. "We rented a condo for the first year in Columbus," Bobby says, "then in '82 Debi took the money I won for being rookie of the year and bought a house,"

He also started playing golf in 1982, developing quickly into a huge golfing enthusiast and playing whenever possible. "I started playing golf when I first got into Indy car racing because CART had so many golf tournaments. I never played it when I was young because I just didn't have any interest in it. But you know, corporate America plays golf, and there's no question that golf has been a benefit to us in terms of finding sponsorship and spending time with people that we wouldn't otherwise have had the opportunity to spend time with."

Besides the camaraderie that golf fosters, Bobby likes the mental challenge of the game. "The thing about golf is that it teases you. One day you play very well, and you can't wait to get out and play the next day. Then you go out the next day and it's like a whole different person playing golf. It's a very rewarding thing when you do get it right and also, by nature of the handicap system, a twenty-one handicapper can play with a scratch golfer and still compete on a friendly basis. I think it's just a great sport."

Bobby started the 1983 season at the Daytona 24 Hours, co-driving Bob Akin's special, purpose-built 935, but the gearbox broke and the car didn't make the start. Meanwhile, Bobby had sold Cribari wine of San Francisco on sponsoring Truesports for the 1983 Indy car season, and the car was turned out in a deep wine red with silver and white trim. Hopes

Tired but happy, Bobby emerges from the car after his first-ever CART victory in Cleveland. (John Krantz II/Rahal collection)

Bobby pushes Thor, the stock-block Chevrolet-powered March, through the Mid-Ohio esses in the September race. Compared with the Cosworth turbo engine, the unturbocharged Chevy provided instant throttle response, which was an advantage on the tight and twisting road course. (Dan Boyd)

At Indianapolis, Bobby is interviewed over the track public address system by veteran announcer Tom Carnegie, who started working as a Speedway announcer in 1945. (Paul Webb)

were high for the team's sophomore year, but the first half of the season was almost a complete bust.

"Cribari was an associate sponsor," Bobby recalls, "except for the California races, when it became the major sponsor. We also did some public service spots with Mothers Against Drunk Driving. Nineteen-eighty-three was a year that we should have achieved a lot of things. We led at Indy for the first time. I think we qualified in the middle, or outside, of the second row, and we holed a radiator, or something insignificant, in the race.

"At Elkhart, we were in the lead and ran out of fuel," Bobby says. "It was really a season of a lot of frustration, although we did win the *L.A. Times* Grand Prix at Riverside, which was a highlight because it was the last race at Riverside for CART, and there was a lot of history to that race and the *L.A. Times* trophy."

Truesports showed its inventiveness that year by building a normally aspirated, stock-block Chevy V-8–powered car for some of the road races. Penske also built a stock-block for one its cars, but Truesports was more successful with its stock-block.

"We found a loophole in the rules and got Franz Weis to build us an engine," Horne recalls. "Lee [Dykstra] drew up the installation for the car, and we ran it at Mid-Ohio."

Says Bobby: "Lee was very good for us, and very good for me. We ended up converting one car to a Chevrolet V-8, because in those days, especially on the road courses, a normally aspirated 350-cubic-inch engine was better than a Cosworth. We were on pole at Mid-Ohio

Bobby's car clouts the wall at Atlanta after a suspension pull-rod broke. The mechanical failure was a result of the high *g*-force loading from the 1.5-mile superspeedway's steep banking. This was the first time Bobby hit the wall on an oval. He was unhurt. (Rich Chenet)

and really should have won going away, but we had a fuel-feed problem in the race and ended up finishing third. I made four pit stops to everybody else's two."

Bobby was on the pole and finished second to Mears at the Michigan 150 in September, but after two disappointing races at Las Vegas and Laguna Seca, he did not start the year's last race at Phoenix following a pit lane crash during the final practice session. Bobby's good friend and personal chief mechanic, Jimmy Prescott, was taken to the hospital with a broken leg and spent most of the winter recovering. Bobby finished the year a disconsolate fifth in the championship behind Al Sr., Teo Fabi, Andretti, and Sneva. "Nineteen-eighty-three was a year when we expected so much more than we achieved for various reasons," Bobby says. "In 1982, we had no expectations and did very well, and that gave us the ammunition to be disappointed in '83."

Bobby also drove a front-engine Ford Mustang GTP car in a couple of IMSA races that year, but the car's little turbocharged four-cylinder engine was overstretched. Bobby finished third at Laguna Seca in May aboard the Mustang and was third again with Geoff Brabham at Elkhart Lake in August. Teammates Klaus Ludwig and Tim Coconis won at Elkhart, but the operation went downhill after that. "That one-three at Elkhart ended up being the highlight of the whole program," Bobby reflects.

Trouble lay in wait in the race at Mid-Ohio. A fuel feed problem meant Bobby had to make twice as many pit stops as everyone else, but he still managed to finish third behind Fabi and Mario Andretti. (Rich Chenet)

"I arrived as a very green race engineer."

After the disappointment of 1983, team owner Trueman attempted to improve the financial and technical strength of Truesports. Bobby and Trueman sold the well-known convenience store chain 7-Eleven on becoming the team's primary sponsor for 1984 and reached agreement with March boss Robin Herd to hire promising young engineer Adrian Newey as the team's race and development engineer. Briefly, toward the end of 1983, Alan Mertens, another March engineer, had replaced the departed Lee Dykstra, but Newey's move to Truesports dramatically increased the strength of Bobby's attack in 1984 and 1985.

An aerodynamicist, Newey had graduated from England's Southampton University in 1980 with a degree in aeronautical engineering, and after an early stint as a draftsman for the failing Fittipaldi F1 team, he went to work for March Engineering in 1982. After one season as a Formula 2 race engineer for former motorcycle racer Johnny Cecotto and another year working on March's GTP car with Al Holbert, Newey was partially involved in designing the March 84C Indy car. He laid out the front suspension and the top of the monocoque, working with chief mechanical designer Mertens and aerodynamicist Ralph Bellamy. "It was

Above: March engineer Adrian Newey was an exciting addition to the Truesports team for the 1984 season. Here he and Bobby ham it up on the pits guardrail at Elkhart Lake. (Christine Horne)

Opposite: On the 1-mile Phoenix oval, Bobby leads Jacques Villeneuve and a knot of cars into turn one. Villeneuve is the brother of Gilles and uncle of Jacques Villeneuve, the 1995 CART Champion and 1997 F1 World Champion. (Bob Tronolone)

Above: Newey discusses setup with Bobby and Jimmy Prescott. Formally trained as an aerody-namicist, Newey pos-sessed an innovative talent that would have a profound influence on the team. (Christine Horne)

Above right: Two impromptu meetings take place late in the day during the Laguna Seca race weekend. Bobby listens to Trueman while Newey listens to Horne. (Christine Horne)

a real committee car, that one," Newey comments. Newey first flew to Columbus in late February of 1984, and it was there that his career really began to take shape.

Today Newey is recognized as one of the world's most accomplished race car designers. He was chief engineer at Williams Grand Prix Engineering, and the cars he designed with the team's technical director, Patrick Head, won F1 World Championships with Nigel Mansell in 1992, Alain Prost in 1993, and Damon Hill in 1996. Newey then joined McLaren in 1997 and became the world's highest-paid race car designer, earning more than $3 million in 1998 as the McLaren F1 team's technical director, and winning the 1998 World Championship with Mika Hakkinen.

Steve Horne comments: "Jim was pushing pretty hard to have a stronger factory relationship with March, so we ended up with Alan Mertens as the team liaison engineer. I think that lasted about three races. Neither Alan, myself, nor Bobby got along, but the following year, in '84, we had Adrian Newey, and that was the start of a very good relationship."

"I arrived as a very green race engineer," Newey recounts. "At that time, Truesports was in a pretty poky little race shop, and I was given a small office in the corner with a very cranky old drawing board, and set about looking at the 1984 Indy car and seeing how it could be improved. To be blunt, that wasn't difficult because, as I said, it was a committee car."

Newey points out that the standard March 84C was oversized and overweight. He tried to reduce its size and modified the bodywork and wings, doing the work without access to a wind tunnel. Aerodynamic modifications he made were track-tested to be certain the changes were actually a step forward. "I had to be fairly careful with what I did, because if you do aerodynamics by eye, it's very easy to go in the wrong direction," Newey notes.

He also tried to get the car down to the weight limit and lowered its center of gravity by angling the engine nose down in the chassis. "That had originally been done principally because of concern over constant-velocity joint angularity, and durability, at the superspeedways, but the superspeedways only made up three or four races. So we reduced

Left: Newey made plenty of changes to Bobby's March, shown here in superspeedway configuration at Indianapolis. He lightened the car and fine-tuned the aerodynamics, suspension geometry, and weight distribution. He also lowered the engine and gearbox. (Dan Boyd)

Below: At the wheel of the Mustang GTP car, Bobby leads the field through the esses at Road Atlanta. Immediately behind are the pair of Group 44 Jaguar XJR5s designed by Lee Dykstra, who worked for Truesports in 1983. (Hal Crocker)

the engine angle, which lowered the whole engine-gearbox assembly, which gave a center-of-gravity height advantage."

The lowered engine and gearbox allowed a new engine cover, which gave cleaner flow to the rear wing, improving aerodynamics as a side benefit. Newey also played around with the suspension geometry and weight distribution. "I think as a result of Bobby's testing feedback and, if you like, my sort of very low-resource, empirical improvements to the car, we actually made a reasonable improvement to the performance of the car compared to a standard off-the-shelf 84C," Newey says.

By the end of the season, the Truesports car had been developed to the level of the Lolas, which had started the season with an advantage over the March. Newey also created a long-wheelbase version of the car for superspeedway races by moving the front suspension forward with the aid of swept-forward wishbones.

Above: From 1984 through 1991, CART races took place on a temporary course set up in the sprawling parking lots of the Meadowlands sports complex in New Jersey. Bobby qualified on the outside pole for the inaugural race in July 1984. (Hal Crocker)

Opposite: At Road America, second-place Bobby celebrates with Mario Andretti (center), who won the race, and Al Unser Sr., who finished third. Bobby overcame a leaking fuel system and low boost pressure to make the podium. (Paul Webb)

Nevertheless, the inexperienced Newey had a lot to learn, particularly about oval racing, but the situation with Rahal and Truesports was perfect and created a blooming educational environment for the young engineer. "The first test I went to was at Phoenix on the oval, and it was pretty much an eye-opener," Newey recalls with a smile. "Having done one season of Formula Two, to turn up at a short oval and try to understand how to engineer the car was a very rapid learning experience, and for that I'll always be very grateful to Bobby in particular, and also to Steve Horne, for their patience in allowing me to find my feet. Basically, they ran the car while I tried to understand what the heck was going on and slowly figured it out. I started to get the hang of it and have enough confidence that I could contribute to the program."

Early in the season, Bobby had made a lot of the engineering and setup recommendations, with Steve Horne contributing as well. Like Newey, they were relatively inexperienced with Indy cars and oval tracks, but they were willing to take Newey's ideas and try them. The openness to fresh thinking at Truesports might have been a difficult environment to find in an older, more established team, Newey believes.

"We undoubtedly made some mistakes," he concedes, "but equally we had a fairly adventurous approach to the whole thing, which could bring new avenues and benefits. Certainly, as I found my feet, Bobby and I started to develop a very close relationship, which, in all honesty, I probably only ever matched once since, with Damon Hill in '96, where we really understood pretty much what we wanted out of the car. Bobby was able to explain to me very precisely what the car was doing. He was very good that way.

"You have to remember this was before telemetry or data acquisition came in. So it was very much, if you like, the hairy-assed approach to race engineering, where you listen to the

driver, go through the circuit, draw a circuit map, discuss the problems the driver's encountering, try to understand those problems, and then come up with solutions."

Once he started to feel more comfortable, Newey found the challenge of CART racing tremendously enjoyable and interesting, particularly the superspeedways. "I think the driver-engineer relationship on the ovals is particularly critical, because it's so precise and requires such fine-tuning, and really, I think Bobby and I developed a very good relationship."

In the middle of the winter, Trueman decided the time had come to build a proper race shop with much more room and facilities. Come spring, the team moved into the new shop, located directly off Interstate 270 in Hilliard, across the highway from Red Roof Inns headquarters.

"Trueman gave us a good shot, both myself and Bobby, in laying out what we wanted," Horne comments. "It was really well presented. That's the building Bobby's in now. Originally, Truesports only had half of it. We moved into there in April of '84, right before Indy. About that time, Trueman was diagnosed with cancer, and that was a bit of a blow to everybody."

Despite Trueman's condition, Horne and the team believed that with Newey on board, they had a realistic chance of challenging for the PPG Cup title. "We felt at the beginning of the year that we could win the championship," Horne declares. "Penske was the number-one opposition, but I think we felt we had a group that was capable of doing it. Certainly Bobby

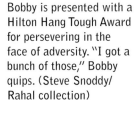

Bobby is presented with a Hilton Hang Tough Award for persevering in the face of adversity. "I got a bunch of those," Bobby quips. (Steve Snoddy/ Rahal collection)

was doing every part of his business. We felt the team had to come up to his level. He was ready to do it before the team was, I think."

For his part, Newey was very impressed with Bobby's driving ability and intellect. "I think Bobby was a well-rounded driver," Newey says. "He was an intelligent driver. He would always think out his strategy during a race. He would push when he needed to, but would hold back when he could get away with holding back. And he very rarely made stupid mistakes.

"I think sometimes his self-preservation meant that he wasn't the bravest driver out there, and occasionally perhaps that hurt him a little bit compared to the ones that really had no fear at all. But the bonus was that because of that, he didn't tend to make silly mistakes and crash out of races."

The year didn't start too well because Bobby was dogged for a few months by mononucleosis. Needless to say, the sickness had an adverse affect on his competitiveness in the opening races at Long Beach and Phoenix. "In March and April of '84 I was literally in bed," Bobby recalls. "I had no energy. I'll never forget, I would sleep so silently, it was almost like I was dead. That really hurt me when we went to Long Beach. That was the first race that year. I was very lackluster, and

Bobby leads Danny Sullivan, Mario Andretti, Michael Andretti, Al Unser, and Josele Garza at the tiny Sanair tri-oval in southern Quebec. Bobby qualified on the pole and finished second to Sullivan and ahead of the senior Andretti. (Paul Webb)

we'd actually gotten up to fourth or fifth when Howdy Holmes and I tangled, and I got taken out of the race."

It was a rough beginning to the season as Bobby dropped out of three of the first five races with transmission-related problems, and at Indianapolis he ran out of fuel and finished three laps behind in seventh place. Bobby began to show seriously competitive form in June at Portland, Oregon, where he led the race until running into gearbox trouble. At the next race, on the frenetic Meadowlands track, Bobby qualified and ran second to Mario Andretti before spinning and stalling.

On the victory podium, Bobby celebrates his win at Phoenix with twenty-something rivals Michael Andretti and Al Unser Jr., who finished third and second, respectively. (Paul Webb)

Then at Cleveland in July, scene of his first win two years earlier, Bobby led, and he fought off a couple of attacks from Andretti and Danny Sullivan. "I was the only March. They were both driving Lolas, and we really had a hell of a fight going on. I finally had broken away from them with five or six laps to go, and the gearbox pitched within sight of the flag. That was one of my bigger disappointments.

"Because of Adrian and our testing, we had slowly done things to the car to make it on par with the Lolas. There was no question that the Lola was the best chassis, at least in the first half of the season in '84, but we ended up winning two races in a row by the end of the year, and should have won more races."

In the Michigan 500, Bobby started from the front row and took the lead in the early laps, and pulled away from the pack. "We had made our last pit stop, and I was within a second or two of Gordon Johncock, who was leading but had yet to stop," Bobby remembers. "Everybody else had to make pit stops except me, and then there was a big accident in front of us.

"During that period you were allowed to put any kind of clunky little brakes on, and Johnny Capels had put little motorcycle-type brakes on Al Holbert's car, and I slowed down, and Holbert couldn't slow down. The next thing I knew, I was in the fence, literally within twenty laps of the flag. We were very fast, and we wrote the car off big time."

At Elkhart Lake, Bobby finally finished, taking second to Andretti despite having to run low boost because of a leaking fuel system. In the Pocono 500 he ran near the front all the way and finished third with a rear tire cut and smoking because of a broken sidepod, crossing the line only a second behind winner Sullivan and second-place Mears.

At Mid-Ohio, Bobby was second behind Andretti. He won his first pole of the year on the frantic, eight-tenths of a mile Sanair tri-oval in Quebec. He led much of that race but had to give best to Sullivan, finishing second with both right-side tires blistered. Bobby was fifth in the Michigan 150 in September. And then he won on both the 1-mile Phoenix oval and the Laguna Seca road course in October. He finished the year third in points, ahead of Sullivan and Mears, but well behind champion Andretti and runner-up Tom Sneva.

"We had turned the car from being a truck into a car that was capable of beating the Lolas," Bobby comments. "I think our March was the only one capable of competing with the Lolas on a regular basis, and that was Adrian's influence and efforts."

The prerace drivers' parade at Sanair with Bobby, the pole winner, at the front, ahead of Sullivan, Roberto Guerrero, Mario and Michael Andretti, and Al Unser. (Paul Webb)

At Laguna Seca the week after Phoenix, Bobby won again. Here he brakes for the Corkscrew, the highest point on the superb Northern California road circuit. (Paul Webb)

Above: On the way to the first of his four straight wins at Laguna Seca, Bobby begins the descent from the Corkscrew, followed by Al Unser Sr. and John Paul Jr. They finished sixth and eleventh, respectively. (Paul Webb)

Above right: On the winner's podium at Laguna with Mario and Michael Andretti, who finished second and third. The late Lee Moselle, who ran Laguna Seca for many years, is at the left in the yellow jacket. (Paul Webb)

Below right: Bobby enjoyed his only race in a NASCAR Winston Cup car at Riverside in November of 1984. He qualified the Wood Brothers Ford in twentieth position at the Southern California road course, but problems with the rear end took him out of the race only 44 laps into the 119-lap event. (Rahal collection)

Newey was relieved to see his driver winning races at last. "To finally get the first win at Phoenix was a milestone," Newey says. "Phoenix and Laguna—that end of the season was rewarding. I think everybody in the team started to have the feeling that we were jinxed, so they were very rewarding wins, but obviously, the championship was long gone by then."

At Sanair in September of 1984, Rick Mears was badly injured when he crashed heavily in practice. Mears's feet and lower legs were crushed almost beyond belief in the accident, and for some time there was doubt about his ability ever to race again. In November of that year, Roger Penske offered Mears's seat to Bobby for 1985, but again Bobby decided to stay with Truesports. As a result, Penske offered the job to Danny Sullivan, who accepted and drove for Penske for six years, from 1985 through 1990.

"Because of my relationship with Jim and because I knew we were in pretty good line to get the Budweiser deal for 1985, I turned down the Penske ride," Bobby explains. "Carl Haas had found bigger sponsorship from Beatrice Foods, and having known Budweiser's sports marketing boss Jack McDonough, who's now with Miller, from the CanAm days when he was with Newman Racing, I just crossed my fingers that Anheuser-Busch would get involved with Truesports."

Early that year Bobby had negotiated a deal with Jaguar's American manager, Mike Dale, to race the whole IMSA season, but Trueman vetoed the idea. "That was one of my great disappointments of that year. I negotiated a hell of a deal. It was great money, and I was really excited about it. Whenever I see Mike I apologize to him, because after I came home and Jim had given me his approval to go ahead with the deal, he told me he didn't

like the idea that I was going to drive something else. He said, what if I got hurt, what if this, or that. I then had to tell Mike that no, I couldn't do it."

Instead, Bobby drove Bruce Leven's Porsche 962, the first of what was then a new generation of Porsche sports cars, in a few races, and also raced a Ford Mustang GTP. Co-driving Leven's 962 with Hurley Haywood, he finished second in that year's Mid-Ohio IMSA race. Bobby also made the only NASCAR Winston Cup appearance of his career that year, driving the Wood Brothers' Ford in the Riverside road race. He qualified twentieth, in the middle of the forty-car field, and ran well until hitting mechanical trouble.

"I qualified halfway up the field, which I thought was pretty fair, considering I didn't know much about driving a Cup car," Bobby relates. "It was a case of not getting the most out of the tires on the first lap of qualifying. After the first lap, the tires were junk. I made a rookie mistake. But the Wood family were just delightful people and went out of their way to make me comfortable. We ran pretty good in the race until the rear end broke."

Settled snugly into the cockpit of the Mustang GTP car. Bobby loved sports car racing and was disappointed the Mustang wasn't more effective. (Hal Crocker)

Bud
VALVOLINE
Bud
GOODYEAR
Bud
3
RED ROOF INNS
GOODYEAR
sleep cheap!
sleep cheap!
DieHard

"We were really building a head of steam."

For 1985, Truesports switched primary sponsors, attracting Budweiser in place of 7-Eleven, as Bobby had hoped. Budweiser had sponsored Mario Andretti and Newman-Haas racing in 1983 and 1984, but Carl Haas found even bigger sponsorship for the new season from Beatrice Foods. Haas recommended Rahal and Truesports to Budweiser, which initiated a very successful four-year relationship. Truesports also hired an additional engineer, Grant Newbury, and an additional manager, Jeff Eischen, who had worked with the Group 44 Jaguar team in IMSA. They also set up a separate test team.

"We were really building a head of steam. We probably had twenty-five people employed in 1985," Horne recalls. "I think because of our relationship with March, and because of Adrian, and because I had always tinkered with the cars, we were always trying to make the car better. Sometimes that was our downfall, I think, but we did a lot of testing and we were strong, particularly at the end of the 1985 season, and Franz was really good with the engines."

Above: Bobby takes a break from winter testing at Laguna Seca to watch the Super Bowl on a television set up in the paddock just behind the pit lane. The driver of an ambulance, which was required to be at the track in case of accident, watches the game with Bobby. (Marc Sproule)

Opposite: Newey incorporated most of the changes he'd made to Bobby's 1984 car into the new March 85C, although some circuit-specific pieces remained proprietary to Truesports. He used proper wind tunnel research to shape the car, but his busy schedule meant others at March had to finish many details. (Paul Webb)

Both Bobby and Newey had shown their talent in 1984, and Newey was duly promoted to chief designer of the 1985 March Indy car. As chief designer, he had to define the concepts and oversee the detail design, fabrication, engineering, and production of more than twenty cars. The new position made Adrian's life busier than ever, as he had to handle two jobs as March's chief designer and Truesports's race engineer.

"It was still a bit of a committee car," Newey says. "I would say I was moderately pleased with it without going so far as to say I was proud of it. Because I was living in the States during the season, race engineering and testing, but had also been put in charge of designing the '85 car by Robin, then I was very much wearing two hats and found it quite difficult to do both properly."

Newey was on a rigorous schedule, flying to England for wind tunnel tests and to supervise the design of the car, then flying back to the States for the next race or test. He believes the design and development of the 1985 March Indy car suffered as a result.

"There was less room for development on the '85 car," Newey says. "I basically took the ideas that I learned working with Truesports on the '84 car into the '85 car." Innovations like the lower engine angle and front suspension tweaks became standard features in the 1985 March customer car, and its aerodynamics were better because they had been Newey's responsibility and were developed in a wind tunnel. Much of the detail work was carried out by other people at March because Newey did not have time to do it himself.

"There were various bits of the '85 car I wasn't really pleased with, particularly the chassis, which was quite cumbersome and high. The top of the chassis was pretty clumsy, which cost us aerodynamically. But nevertheless, it was a car that was good enough. It had a bit of an edge over the '85 Lola."

Newey also designed a few special pieces strictly for Truesports. "We did some different front and rear wings, and there was a further modification of the front suspension. In '84, we were the first to try long wheelbase for the superspeedways." Newey and Herd agreed that the modifications for certain track configurations that Newey had developed with Truesports would stay proprietary, for Truesports alone.

"Things like the long wheelbase I considered circuit-dependent, because we'd only run that at the superspeedways. So that wasn't standard on the '85 car, but I did a set of long-wheelbase front suspension for Truesports's '85 car for Indy."

Much like the previous year, the 1985 season started poorly, with Bobby finishing only once in the first six races, although he qualified well at almost every race. He was on the pole in five of the last six races and was on the outside of the front row in the other race. He took his first pole of the year at Cleveland and was fastest again in qualifying for the Michigan 500—only to crash in a subsequent practice session due to a tire failure. Consequently, he started his backup car from

Left: Bobby was seriously into golf by this stage of his life. "This was the first time I played the AT&T Pro-Am tournament at Pebble Beach. I'm with Roger [Penske] and professional golfers Danny Edwards [who also races Formula Fords as a hobby] and Jeff Sluman." (Rahal collection)

Below: At Indianapolis, Bobby qualified on the outside of the front row, but once again he failed to finish after dropping out before half-distance with turbo waste-gate problems. (Dan Boyd)

the tail of the field. Things finally came right at Mid-Ohio, the team's home track, where Bobby won convincingly after starting from the pole.

Bobby finished the year with a flourish, winning from the pole in the Michigan 150 and at Laguna Seca. At Sanair, he led strongly from the pole before tangling with Jacques Villeneuve, the younger brother of the great Gilles and uncle of the 1995 Indy 500 winner and 1997 World Champion, Jacques Villeneuve. Bobby was trying to lap Villeneuve at the time, but the local hero would not give way, and they collided heavily in the first turn. Bobby climbed out of his wrecked car and waved a fist at Villeneuve while Horne ran down from Truesports's pit to rudely berate the local man.

Once again, Bobby finished third in the championship, ahead of Andretti and Sullivan but behind the dueling father-and-son pair, Al Unser and Al Unser Jr. Al Sr. won only once that year, at Phoenix in October, but outscored everyone with consistent finishes, beating his son by just one point. Rahal was another sixteen points behind in third and was only too aware that the crash with Villeneuve in Quebec had cost him the title.

"In 1985 we had a lot of poles and won three times, and probably should have won a few more," Bobby says. "If Jacques Villeneuve hadn't hit me at Sanair, we would have won the championship that year. We would have won it three years in a row.

"We had a lot of great races. At Cleveland we had pole, and one of the mechanics had rebuilt the clutch master cylinder the night before the race and put it in backward. I went out, and it slipped right from the word go. It only lasted a couple of laps.

"There were some disappointments that year, but in terms of the confidence I had with Adrian, much of it stemmed from '84. But in '85 our communication was perfect. It was almost as if he knew what I was thinking. I'd say something, and he'd know exactly what I meant."

Bobby also finished third in the 1985 IROC series, scoring an excellent win at his home course, Mid-Ohio. And he won that year's Elkhart Lake IMSA race, driving Rob Dyson's Budweiser Porsche 962 with Drake Olson. "It was a great race because it started to rain and I stayed out on slicks," Bobby says, "and we just killed 'em because it didn't get that bad, and you were able to go as fast on slicks as on rain tires, and we were able to make one less pit stop than everybody else."

At the end of 1985, much to Bobby's dismay, Newey departed Truesports to take over the race engineer's job with Maury Kraines's Kraco team. "I think various factors came in there," Newey explains. "Steve ran a pretty tight ship in all senses of the word, really. I think he and Robin [Herd], that relationship was not as strong as it could have been. I think various things happened at once."

Opposite: After threatening to win all year, Bobby finally pulled it off at Mid-Ohio, the tenth race of the season. He led all the way from the pole. Here track and team owner Trueman congratulates Bobby before the start of the victory circle ceremonies. Newey stands at the front of the car. (Paul Webb)

Below: Bobby takes the lead from the outside of the front row at the start at Phoenix in October. Leading the chase are Emerson Fittipaldi (40), pole and race winner Al Unser (5), and Danny Sullivan (4). Bobby finished sixth. (Paul Webb)

One of those things, Newey thinks, was that Herd saw business potential to develop with Kraines, and as part of that, Kraines had to feel that he was the works team. An important component of that relationship was providing Newey, who was responsible for the design of the car, as the Kraco team's engineer.

"From my side, I very much respected Steve, and I also wanted to stay working with Bobby, but Steve was being fairly inflexible with the salary offer, which, compared to what other engineers in Indy cars were earning, was fairly low. While money is never my principal motivator, it was an insult that he wasn't prepared to move beyond an extra $5,000 he offered for the following year.

"The other thing with Kraco, and this to me was the biggest single factor," Newey adds, "was I wanted to be in a position to move into Formula One at some stage in the near future. That meant that by the middle of the year I needed to be free to reduce my Indy commitments so that I could start concentrating on the design of a Formula One car for whatever F1 team I joined, should there be an opportunity. If I was going to move to Formula One, it was only going to be in a position of responsibility; in other words, as the chief designer of that team.

"Steve was insisting that if I was going to be their engineer, I had to do the whole season, including tests, or nothing. Maury Kraines, with Robin's persuasion, no doubt, was prepared to accept that I would do ten races, which basically meant if I did the first half of the season I'd only have to do a couple more races thereafter. So all those factors, and I think principally the latter, meant that, regrettably, I felt it was time to move on."

So Newey went to work designing the March 86C Indy car and joined the Kraco team to work as race engineer for Michael Andretti, who would battle fiercely with Bobby for the

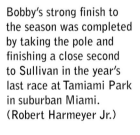

Bobby's strong finish to the season was completed by taking the pole and finishing a close second to Sullivan in the year's last race at Tamiami Park in suburban Miami. (Robert Harmeyer Jr.)

1986 PPG Cup championship. In the middle of the year, much as he had hoped, Newey joined Carl Haas's new Beatrice-Force F1 team as a designer and race engineer. But by the end of the year, amid a corporate reorganization, Haas lost his giant Beatrice sponsorship and closed the doors of his F1 team after the Beatrice conglomerate was purchased by leveraged-buyout experts Kohlberg, Kravis, Roberts. Newey stayed with Haas in 1987, working as Mario Andretti's race engineer for the Newman-Haas CART team, before joining the Leyton House–March F1 team for 1988 and 1989, then moving on with great success to Williams in 1990 and then to McLaren in 1997.

In the meantime, Bobby was devastated by Newey's departure from Truesports. "Probably one of the greatest disappointments of my life was when Adrian went off to Kraco," Bobby declares. "We ended up winning the championship in '86, but at the end of '85, looking into the new year, I felt that we were taking a step backward. Adrian had been such a major force, and when he didn't continue with us, I felt that was a big blow."

Bobby's admiration for Newey's talent remains huge. "The thing that made Adrian so great to me is his intuitiveness. Yes, he's book smart, but he's the kind of guy that can wet his finger and see which way the wind is blowing and react to it. There are a lot of engineers that are book smart, but intuitiveness, I think, is what makes an engineer great.

"At some point you've got to shut the computers off and look outside and see what's going on, and that's where Adrian, I think, is so brilliant. His ability to grab hold of the moment, understand what the issues are, and find a solution. And for a driver, man, you think you're Superman when you've got somebody like that on your side."

"We were supposed to run a Ferrari in '87."

In 1985, Rahal and Truesports had begun to approach the zenith of their '80s performance. That year, Bobby had started from the front row ten times, took five poles, and won four of the season's last six races. For the second year in a row he was third in the championship, closing rapidly over the final races on Al Unser Sr. who beat his son, Al Jr., to the title by one point. By this time, Bobby and Truesports were acknowledged to be among the best in the business, and many new doors were beginning to open.

Early in 1985, an intriguing, experimental relationship developed between Truesports and Ferrari. At the time, Ferrari was embroiled in one of many fierce political battles the company has had with motor racing's international ruling body, the FIA. Ferrari was threatening to quit Formula One and race Indy cars in America instead unless some changes were made in the way the FIA administered Formula One. To back up its saber rattling, Ferrari needed to demonstrate at least some intent to switch to Indy cars. It did so by co-opting Bobby and one of Truesports's March-Cosworths for some secret testing at its Fiorano test track, then proceeding to design and build an Indy car and engine.

Above: The Ferrari Indy car was never raced, and no photos have ever been published from the one occasion that it was driven by Michele Alboreto. Although its design drew from the proven March Indy car, the Ferrari clearly has a look all its own. The engine cover appears sleeker and longer than the Lola, March, and Penske Indy cars of the time. (Ferrari S.p.A.)

Opposite: In 1985, the head man in Formula One, FIA vice president Bernie Ecclestone, proposed limiting F1 engines to eight cylinders. This idea was anathema to Enzo Ferrari, whose engines were traditionally twelve cylinders. He threatened to withdraw from F1 and race in CART instead. (Ferrari S.p.A.)

Because of Ferrari's association with Goodyer as both its F1 and original equipment production car tire supplier, the Italian manufacturer asked Goodyear's Leo Mehl to recommend a CART team to work with to explore Indy car racing. Mehl had been Goodyear's racing manager for twenty years, and he wielded considerable power and earned commensurate respect during his two decades in command of motorsport's most broad-based and influential tire maker. With Rahal and Truesports on a rapid rise in CART, Mehl did not hesitate to provide the strongest possible recommendation on their behalf to Ferrari.

Steve Horne explains how the Ferrari episode took place. "We were approached by Leo Mehl," Horne recalls. "So we went over to Ferrari with Jim in extreme secrecy and made a deal to help them. At the end of '85 we sent a car over there for three weeks. They tested it, pulled it apart, and looked at everything they needed to on the dyno."

Bobby has similar memories of the Ferrari affair. "This was right in the middle of the racing season, and I went over there to test in September, while the racing season was still going on. We had a skeleton crew over there, and we tried to convince Adrian to leave March and design the Ferrari Indy car, but we didn't know March had committed Adrian to Kraco for 1986."

What followed for Bobby and the team was an unprecedented time of secret testing and Machiavellian strategies. Enzo Ferrari's son, Piero Lardi, was put in charge of the project, and CART's series sponsor, PPG Industries, got involved in serious discussions about spon-

Ferrari engineers closely examined the Truesports March-Cosworth that Bobby tested at Fiorano, the company's test track in northern Italy. Subsequently Ferrari went to work designing and building its own car, the Type 637, and engine, the Type 034. Gustav Brunner was chief designer. (Ferrari S.p.A.)

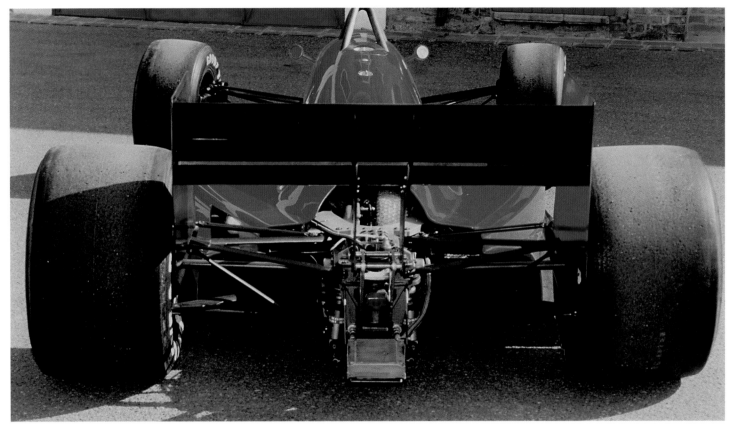

soring the Ferrari Indy car. With Newey unavailable, Ferrari decided to hire Austrian designer Gustav Brunner to design its Indy car.

"Gustav was a great guy," Bobby says, "and he came to a lot of our races in 1985. Then we went and tested our March-Cosworth at Fiorano, and [Michele] Alboreto drove the car a little bit. Of course, Ferrari copied everything, or tried to.

"I remember us having dinner with Piero Lardi at a Cooker's," Bobby goes on. "I couldn't believe that Jim [Trueman] was going to take Piero Lardi to a Cooker's restaurant, which is like going to a Friday's, you know? That was so typical of Jim. He wasn't awed by anybody.

"A few weeks later," Bobby continues, "we started testing at the track, which is all walled in, and pretty soon noticed a few heads climbing a few telephone poles to watch. It was so typically Italian. I ran two days, and it was a lot of fun. Just like Varano in '78."

Bobby's rare inside look at Ferrari's research and development operation convinced him that the Italian manufacturer enjoyed unmatched commitment in money and resources. "One of the things that was amazing was there were stacks of engines in the area of the shop where the Indy car was," he recalls. "There were V-6s, V-8s, V-12s, in-line sixes, in-line fours, stacked up literally by the hundreds. They had been run once or twice, tested, and

Above: A feature of Ferrari's stillborn Type 637 was a transverse gearbox with the gear clusters going across the car rather than being situated in the direction of travel. Transverse 'boxes have been employed at different times by various Champ car designers but have never supplanted the more traditional longitudinal transmissions. (Ferrari S.p.A.)

thrown away. I remember walking out of there and thinking it's amazing that anyone can compete with that kind of might. When they were making a design change, it wasn't a little of this or that, it was, 'Let's change the vee angle and build a whole new engine.' "

After the test, Bobby took his Truesports mechanics with him on a sightseeing trip and discovered that being a tourist doesn't mix with Ferrari-style secrecy. "We went down to Florence," Bobby remembers. "I wanted to give them the benefit of my local knowledge from my Formula Three and Two days. We did the sights and the galleries and walked along the piazza, did the whole thing.

The Ferrari Indy engine finally saw the light of day in 1989, when an iteration of the prototype 034 engine was raced for the first time as an Alfa Romeo. The Alfa brand is also owned by Ferrari's parent company, Fiat. (Dan Boyd)

"Well, I had to get Debi something, so I go into a Gucci store, and who do I run smack into but Jim Williams, who was over there on vacation. It was like, 'What are you doing here? Well, what are *you* doing here?' I also ran into Masten Gregory that same day. It was amazing." Williams and Gregory had links with two of Bobby's biggest rivals in CART. A food wholesaler and race car collector, Williams was and is associated with Roger Penske, while Gregory, who passed away a few years later, was a retired F1 and sports car racer from Chicago who was close to Carl Haas.

Ultimately, the Ferrari episode came to nothing, apparently a political ruse of the finest kind, but Ferrari certainly spent a lot of time and money on the experimental project. "In the end," Bobby notes, "Enzo was just pulling everybody's chain. He was fighting with the FIA, as he did so often. But it was an interesting time and an interesting experience."

Steve Horne adds to Bobby's recollection. "There was some question as to whether the relationship would keep going," Horne comments, "but Ferrari stayed with it, and we continued to work with them in '86. They ultimately built a car. The car ran, although Bobby never drove it. I think Alboreto drove it. That was right at the time John Barnard was going to Ferrari, and he told the Old Man quite rightly, 'Get one thing right, then move on to the next thing.' So that was the end of that deal, but theoretically we were supposed to run a Ferrari in '87. That was an extremely interesting time."

Ironically, four years later Ferrari's turbo V-8 Indy engine was resurrected and carried the Alfa Romeo nameplate. Like Ferrari, Alfa is owned by the giant Fiat group, and from 1989 through 1991 the rebadged Ferrari engine raced in CART and at Indianapolis. It was conspicuously unsuccessful, however, and ran at the tail of the field despite top drivers like Al Unser Sr. and Danny Sullivan. The engine's power output was never within 100 horsepower of the competition.

Alfa Romeo's last two dismal seasons in Indy car racing were shared with veteran CART owner Pat Patrick's team. So poor was the performance of the engines that the episode all but finished the careers of Unser and Sullivan, and ultimately left Patrick looking for a buyer for his team at the end of 1991.

Danny Sullivan led the Alfa effort in 1991 in a Patrick Racing–Miller Lola. Sullivan was fourth in Australia and fifth at Milwaukee, but by season's end, Fiat and Alfa Romeo had pulled the plug on the program. (Dan Boyd)

"I don't remember crossing the finish line!"

After nearly two years, Jim Trueman was losing his battle with cancer. Trueman for most of his life was a fit, healthy person who loved sports and physical activity. He had built Red Roof Inns into a booming business and was an informal, sharp-witted man who was a welcome and valued addition to CART's often fractious team-owning board of directors. As 1986 began, it was clear Trueman was fighting for his life.

At the same time, Bobby and Horne made a serious effort at a stronger start to the new season than in previous years. "Going into 1986, I think Bobby and I both sat down and said, 'We need to concentrate on getting out of the blocks better,' " Horne says.

"So we managed to get the '86 March quite early. We did quite a bit of testing. Adrian had been poached away from us by Robin Herd. So we decided, almost by accident, because he was there, to promote Grant Newbury to be race engineer, and it turned out to be a great success story.

Above: Jim Trueman joins Debi and Bobby on the victory lap at Indianapolis in the Corvette pace car. This win was the crowning achievement in Trueman's long racing career. (Rich Chenet)

Opposite: Bobby takes the traditional swig of milk in victory lane at Indianapolis. For Bobby, the jubilation of the win was offset by the knowledge that Trueman would soon die. Christine Horne, with her back to the camera, stands to the left at the front of the car. (Rahal collection)

"Grant came in with a pretty fresh mind. He'd been with us a couple of years. He'd seen what Adrian had done, and we just really concentrated on the basics, and the basic things that were wrong with the car, a little cooling and waste-gate problems. We really tried to make them correct, and we were rolling. There was no stopping us."

Before the Indy car season started, Bobby had planned to race one of the new BMW-bankrolled and powered March GTP cars in the Daytona 24 Hours and Sebring 12 Hours. He had convinced Trueman the March-BMW program was worth doing, but it quickly turned into a debacle.

"I arrived at Daytona after taking a red-eye all night from Laguna, where I'd been testing the Indy car," Bobby says. "I got there just in time for a press conference announcing the team's withdrawal because the car had burned to the ground in practice." The fire had been caused by a fuel leak.

"Then we went to Sebring, and I'm driving this thing, and I couldn't believe the power it had! In the first practice session I was a ridiculous amount faster than everyone else, and in qualifying I was just cruising, getting ready for a qualifying lap. Then I started to go for it, and in the fast left-hander after the pits, I went through there flat."

As Bobby blazed through the first turn, the ill-fitting rear bodywork came off, taking the wing and everything else with it. Bobby was in for a wild ride: "So I'm sliding across the road, and it's going, *Bam! Bam! Bam!* And then nothing. Everything goes quiet, and I'm upside down. Then it comes down and goes, *Bang! Bang! Bang!* It was like you hit and wait for a while, then hit and wait for a while. It must have gone on for 500 yards. It went from turn two to turn three, and the thing ends up upside down, and I'm in there and I can smell fuel dripping.

"I was in a hurry to get out," Bobby continues, "and I forgot that once you undo your safety belts and you're hanging upside down, that you're gonna go, boom, into the roof. And I hit the ground, headfirst. It stunned me a bit, but I scrambled out of there as fast as I could." It was the biggest accident he had had up to that point in his career.

Below: The number-12 March-BMW was the sister car to the one Bobby had planned to race at Daytona and Sebring. At Daytona, Bobby's car went up in flames before he arrived, and at Sebring, this car, driven by David Hobbs and John Watson, was also withdrawn because it caught fire. (Lee Self)

Below right: With its mechanical pieces largely hidden beneath a packing blanket, the remains of Bobby's March BMW is moments away from being loaded into its transporter. The crash was a huge one, by far the largest of Bobby's career up to that point. Note the broken bodywork in the foreground. (Lee Self)

The first two races of the Indy car season, Phoenix and Long Beach, were essentially nonevents, as Bobby qualified in the midfield and failed to finish both races. But at Indianapolis, he qualified on the inside of the second row and was in the hunt all the way on race day. Through the month of May, it became clear that Trueman did not have long to live, but the man's spirit miraculously drove him on to survive through race day at Indianapolis. In fact, the race was delayed six days because of rain, but Trueman was there nevertheless to witness the ultimate realization of his dream as Bobby won the seventieth running of the 500, beating Kevin Cogan and Rick Mears in a classic late-race shoot-out.

"We won Indy, which was obviously a big thrill, and a big disappointment because of Jim's condition," Horne says. "Bobby was really driving well. You couldn't have asked for any more. He was smooth and fast, and the quality of his race craft had gone to another level."

Bobby qualified on the inside of the second row and ran all the way with leaders Rick Mears and Michael Andretti. He led about a quarter of the race and near the end was running second behind Kevin Cogan and ahead of Mears when Arie Luyendyk crashed. That brought out the race's last caution flag with just six laps to go. Four laps were run under the yellow before the starter waved the green flag with just two laps left.

Bobby takes the checkered flag at Indianapolis in front of the packed grandstands. He was so intent on his dwindling fuel supply and willing his car through the last lap that he doesn't remember this historic moment. (Rich Chenet)

In what has become a famous story, ABC television commentator Sam Posey asked Cogan over a radio link to comment on the restart as Cogan led the field through the third turn on the approach to the green flag. "I'm kind of busy right now, Sam," Cogan replied as he tried to outfox Bobby by accelerating hard, then jumping off the throttle. Cogan hoped Bobby would have to back off or brake and lose momentum, but Bobby played it perfectly, getting the jump on Cogan and passing him for the lead as they ran flat out toward the first turn.

"I knew if I could go into turn one with the lead, no one could probably get by me again in less than two laps," Bobby says. He beat Cogan and Mears away from the restart and held on to win by a few car lengths, worrying all the way to the checkered flag about running out of fuel. "I can remember the last few laps as clearly today as if it was yesterday," Bobby says. "The fuel light was blinking the last two laps, and I knew Mears and I were tight on fuel. I was going down the back straight on the last lap, and I was screaming, 'Don't leave me! Don't leave me! Don't leave me now, baby!' Just like a jockey. And I don't remember crossing the finish line!"

After the race, Trueman, emaciated but smiling warmly, was driven around the historic track beside Bobby and Debi aboard the pace car on a poignant victory lap. When Bobby called his father after winning Indy to tell him the news, Mike's reaction was immediate and characteristically pragmatic. "We had started building a new house in Muirfield Village in

In the grip of terminal cancer, Trueman willed himself to return to Indianapolis a week after the rain-out to be there for the seventieth running of the 500. Ten days after Bobby's victory, Trueman passed away. He was fifty-one. (Dan Boyd)

The New York Times

SPORTS

Section **5**

Sunday, June 1, 1986

Rahal Wins Indy 500 in Closest Three-Car Finish

Cogan Is 2d And Mears 3d

By FRANK LITSKY
Special to The New York Times

INDIANAPOLIS, May 31 — Bobby Rahal made one lightning move with two laps to go today and won the 70th, richest and fastest Indianapolis 500.

With six laps remaining in the 200-lap race, 30-year-old Kevin Cogan of Redondo Beach, Calif., was leading; 33-year-old Rahal of Dublin, Ohio, was second, and 34-year-old Rick Mears of Bakersfield, Calif., the qualifying leader, third. One was close behind the other. Then the yellow flag came out for a minor accident.

That meant that the leaders' speed of 200 or miles an hour had to be reduced to 120 to 150, and no car could pass another. Had the yellow flag stayed up, the race would have ended with that order.

"If the green flag didn't come out," said Rahal, "there would have been a mutiny in the grandstands."

There was no mutiny. With two laps remaining, the green flag came out, and the day came down to a three-car, two-lap race. As the leaders passed the start-finish line, building up to maximum speed, Rahal dived for the inside. He got in front or Cogan and held on to the checkered flag. Rahal, driving the Budweiser/Truesports March with a Cosworth V-8 en-

1985," Bobby recounts, "and I'll never forget when we won Indy, my mother was there, but my dad had had back surgery and couldn't be there. So I called him up to say, 'Dad, do you believe it?' And he said the only thing he could think of was, 'You can buy your house now.' It was a typical father's comment."

Trueman was able to join his team to celebrate the great victory that evening. Ten days later he died at home in Columbus. Those were extremely bittersweet days for everyone at Truesports as the team reached the crescendo of its achievement, only to be faced with the death of its founder and mentor.

"I think we were all in shock," Bobby says about Trueman's death. "We were all trying to deal with Jim's death in our own ways and not let it get in the way of what we knew he expected us to do. He was our leader, almost a father to many of us. We missed him tremendously."

Horne admits there was no plan in place for Truesports when Trueman died. "I think by the time we got to Indy, everybody knew he wasn't going to survive," Horne says. "But he was

Following pages: An ecstatic Steve Horne greets Bobby as he heads down the pit road after the cool-off lap toward victory lane. This was the first of six wins Bobby would score that year on his way to the 1986 PPG Cup championship. (Dan Boyd)

145

THIS AREA RESTRICTED TO
TWO MEN PER CAR

RED ROOF INN

Bud
KING OF BEERS

CHAMPION

3

Budweiser

DieHard

STP

GOODYEAR

the kind of guy who never said, 'Hey, when I die, we're going to do this, this, and this.' He just sort of died, and Bobby and I kinda looked at each other and said, 'What do we do now?'

"Barbara [Trueman] sent over a couple of attorneys from Red Roof and told us we were going to keep going, but I think when we lost Jim, we lost someone who had given us an opportunity and who had such a unique style of managing people. He was at times very standoffish, letting you get on with the job, and other times, right when you needed it, he'd give you the encouragement and the direction to keep going. So it was a big personal blow, I think. But Jim's death came in the middle of the season, so we had something to focus on—to continue racing.

"I think, looking back," Horne adds, "if we hadn't had the Budweiser sponsorship, the doors would have shut that day. I don't think there was the will on Barbara's part to keep going, and that showed later on. But we had racing to keep us going."

Through the next four races, Bobby struggled, failing to finish two of them and taking sixth at Milwaukee and third at the Meadowlands in New York. Then in July, in the first race run through the streets of downtown Toronto's Exhibition

Place, Bobby qualified on the front row and won, beating Sullivan and Mario Andretti despite a penalty for passing the pace car.

"I think Toronto was the most important race for us to win that year," Bobby comments. "After Jim passed away, there were a lot of questions about the future of the team, and in terms of morale, I think everything could have folded very easily if we hadn't been able to win another race very soon. But to win in Toronto in almost an easy way, well, it really turned things around for them, for everyone involved, at a critical stage."

After winning in Toronto, Bobby won four more races, including three in a row at Mid-Ohio, Sanair, and Michigan, as well as his third win in three years at Laguna Seca. He beat twenty-four-year-old Michael Andretti for the 1986 PPG Cup, catching and passing Andretti in the season's second half, then beat him by eight points at a time when Michael was at the height of his youthful aggression with Maury Kraines's March, engineered by Adrian Newey.

"At one point, we won five of eight races," Bobby remarks. "We won three in a row, and of course, we didn't have Adrian. Michael had Adrian. The championship came down to the last race, but we outqualified him. Their car broke, and ours didn't."

Bobby gives Horne a lot of credit for stepping into the void left by Trueman and keeping the team's effort focused and together. "Instead of gnashing our teeth and wringing our hands and saying the end is near, we got down to business. If there's one thing Steve Horne was always good at it is that he was always very much of a realist and a pragmatist. You understood very clearly that whether things were in your favor or not, you were going to keep working, keep going forward."

At Phoenix in October, Bobby qualified on the pole and finished third behind Michael Andretti and Danny Sullivan. Only one race remained—Miami—and by that stage of the year, Andretti was the only driver with a mathematical chance of beating Bobby to the championship. (Dan Boyd)

That year Bobby also raced an IMSA Ford Probe GTP car a few times, at Miami early in the year and at Elkhart Lake and Columbus later in the season. Competitive as the Probe was, it didn't finish any of the races Bobby started. "Budweiser sponsored part of it, but it just didn't pay off. The car didn't last long in any of the races," Bobby says.

At the end of 1986, Bobby and Horne visited Lola Cars and decided the time was ripe to switch from running March to Lola chassis. "Our reason for moving to Lola," Horne says, "was that Robin Herd was diversifying March very rapidly, and the resources weren't there to support the CART program. We thought he was taking his eye off the ball a lot. Whereas each year you could see Lola getting better and better."

Conversations with Lola's chief designer, Nigel Bennett, in particular convinced Bobby and Horne that Lola was the way to go for 1987. "Nigel Bennett had been there a couple of years," Horne recalls. "He was a real quiet guy but a sleeper as far as a designer. So we went and took a look, and we decided to switch to Lola, which turned out to be a stroke of either luck or genius because the March 87C was a pig, and the 1987 Lola was the car to have."

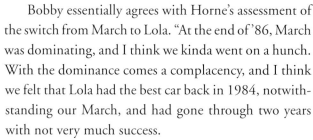

Ford's IMSA racing manager, Preston Miller, talks with Bobby and Tom Gloy at the Columbus IMSA race in October. "Gloy and I used to have bets about which early flight we would catch on race day because the engines in the Mustang GTP car never lasted," Bobby says. Gloy is now Bobby's partner in a NASCAR truck team. (Dan Boyd)

Bobby essentially agrees with Horne's assessment of the switch from March to Lola. "At the end of '86, March was dominating, and I think we kinda went on a hunch. With the dominance comes a complacency, and I think we felt that Lola had the best car back in 1984, notwithstanding our March, and had gone through two years with not very much success.

"I just really felt that when you talked to Nigel Bennett and to Eric Broadley and Mike Blanchet at Lola, there was no question that maybe they had tried to cut corners in 1985 and '86, or been complacent, but in 1987 they weren't going to do that. We looked brilliant in hindsight, because the '87 March was nothing more than a warmed-up '86, whereas the '87 Lola was a totally different race car. Really, I think the '87 Lola is what set the modern-day Champ car onto the path that it is on today. I mean, compared to an '85 or '86 Champ car, it was a much smaller car. It was a great car."

With his new Lola chassis, Bobby won three races in 1987, finished second five times, and added two third places—ten podiums—to beat Michael Andretti to the championship for the second year in a row. This time Michael was thirty points behind, and third-place Al Unser

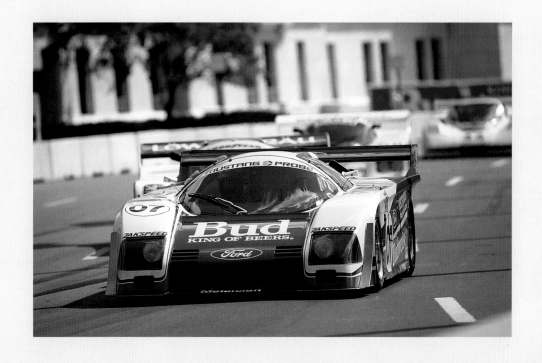

Left: The Budweiser-sponsored Probe in action at Columbus. Fast but with fragile engines, the car didn't finish any of the races Bobby entered. This particular example of the Probe was powered by a Ford-Cosworth DFL, an enlarged version of the DFV F1 engine. (Dan Boyd)

Below: Bobby practices in the rain at the Tamiami season-closer. He finished eighth in the race and clinched the 1986 CART championship. Bobby won almost $1.5 million in 1986. He was the first CART driver to win more than a million in a single season. (Jon Eisberg)

Jr. trailed in the dust another fifty points back. Bobby led fewer laps that year than either Michael or Mario Andretti but finished more races.

Both Andrettis battled unreliable engines in 1987. Michael raced development Cosworth engines, built at the Kraco team's headquarters in southern California, while Mario lost race after race, Indy 500 included, in his first year racing Ilmor's new Chevrolet Indy V-8. Franz Weis's more conservative but ultrareliable Cosworth V-8 turbos were worth their weight in gold that year to Bobby and Truesports.

Bobby rates his victory over Mario and Michael Andretti at the Meadowlands that summer as not only his best race that year but one of the best of his life. "People ask me what are the most memorable or satisfying races, and to me that was one of my most satisfying races ever, beating Mario at the Meadowlands that year. It was a horrible racetrack, and Mario was at his height with Newman-Haas. He had a Lola-Ilmor, and I had a Lola-Cosworth. It was a very, very hot and humid day, and I had about a 10-second lead, and a yellow came out with ten laps to go, and my lead evaporated. And there was Mario right behind me, but I pulled out about 5 seconds over the last ten laps and I beat him.

"That to me was very satisfying. I had invested so much respect in Mario, and he had so much international credibility. If it had been anybody else, the satisfaction wouldn't have been as great, but to beat Mario Andretti meant something.

"Toronto was another very good race for us in 1987," Bobby says. "We finished third because of a faulty brake caliper, but while the car was running well, I don't think anybody was faster than us. The Michigan 500 in 1987 was also a good race, coming from three laps behind

Opposite: Elkhart Lake was the only race in the second half of the 1987 season that Bobby failed to finish. "The car was really handling well; it was hooked up, and we were just taking it easy. Then the turbocharger broke," Bobby says. "It happened pretty early in the race." He had started fourth. (Rich Chenet)

Left: Bobby wrapped up his second championship in a row by scoring his fourth straight win at Laguna Seca. Here he descends from the Corkscrew through the trees. Danny Sullivan finished second, and Rick Mears was third. (Dan Boyd)

"Sebring was one of my most meaningful victories because of Sebring's historic value and what the race meant to me personally," Bobby says. In victory lane at Sebring, he and Mass share the celebration with Leven's delighted team. (Art Flores)

to finish on the same lap. But I would definitely say the best race for me as a driver was the Meadowlands. Nobody had any excuses that day. We just flat-out beat Mario and Michael."

Bobby also ran six IMSA races in 1987, winning three of them and finishing second twice and third in the other race so that he was fifth in the IMSA championship despite running only a third of the season. He drove one of Bruce Leven's pair of Bayside-Texaco Porsche 962s in IMSA, winning at Sebring and Mid-Ohio with Jochen Mass, and scoring a solo victory at Columbus. An IMSA street race was run in downtown Columbus for four years, from 1985 through 1988, and Bobby rates his victory in his adopted hometown in 1987 as another one of his best races. In the closing laps of a long race, he passed teammate Mass to win.

"I passed Jochen with about five laps to go in the hairpin in a place where he wasn't expecting it. That was a two-and-a-half-hour street race, a hard race. I passed Jochen for the lead where nobody thought you could pass. I just got beside him and he wasn't looking and had to give way. That was a good win for us, especially here in Columbus."

June had been an impressive month for Bobby, as he won four races: an International Race of Champions (IROC) race at Mid-Ohio, an IMSA race at Mid-Ohio, and the Portland and Meadowlands CART races.

"My only disappointment that year was I led the Mid-Ohio CART race all the way, and my impatience got the best of me. I was lapping [Rick] Miskawiecz, and he knocked me out of the race with about three laps to go. I ended up second. That would have been three in a row at Mid-Ohio. It was just stupid. But we won a lot of races in 1986 and '87."

At Del Mar, three weeks after winning in Columbus, Bobby fought transmission problems to finish third. "I lost the clutch, and the 962 had a synchromesh transmission, so I had to be slow with all my shifts and match revs when I was downshifting," Bobby remembers. (Marc Sproule)

At the end of the year, Bobby added the inaugural Marlboro Challenge to his list of victories. A special, big-dollar sprint race run on Saturday at the season closer in Tamiami Park on the outskirts of Miami, the Marlboro Challenge paid $225,000 to the winner, helping Bobby's income for the year to again top the million-dollar mark.

In 1987, Truesports jelled as a team and together with the new car made a formidable combination that rival teams could not equal. "The Lola was reliable, easy to set up, and Grant was engineering it," Horne says. "We just walked it. We won the championship easily. At Indy, we had a little problem with the throttle linkage, which was disappointing, but we just smoked it.

"I remember at one race, everybody was complaining that we must be cheating. We were being accused of using a tire-softening compound, and I remember one of Penske's guys coming up and cutting a little piece off one of our tires during tech inspection and sticking it in his pocket. I think everybody was convinced we had some sort of secret device, or weapon, when really it was just the combination of Bobby, me, and the guys."

The Truesports team was at the peak of its performance when it won its second championship in 1987. Bobby finished on the podium ten times, and Truesports had a cohesiveness that no other team could match. This team photo was taken at Indianapolis in May. (Christine Horne collection)

"It was a disappointing end to a long relationship."

As successful as 1986 and 1987 had been for Bobby and Truesports, the seeds of dissolution were sown towards the end of Bobby's second championship season. As 1987 unfolded, it became increasingly clear that the Ilmor-Chevrolet engine, first raced by Penske Racing in 1986, was coming into its own. Mario Andretti scored the Ilmor-Chevy's first win in the 1987 season opener at Long Beach, California, and the engine won five races that year to Cosworth's ten victories, of which six were by Bobby. But it was obvious the Ilmor engine outpowered Cosworth's venerable DFX and by season's end, most CART teams were scrambling to either switch to Chevrolet or find some other engine to replace the aging DFX.

Ilmor is located in central England, only 15 miles from Cosworth. Today Ilmor builds Mercedes-Benz's Formula One and Champ car engines. The company was founded in 1984 by former Cosworth engineers Mario Ilien and Paul Morgan, in partnership with Roger Penske and Chevrolet. The first Ilmor-Chevrolet Indy engine appeared in 1986 and was

Above: The Ilmor-Chevy was first raced in 1986 by Al Unser Sr. It was powerful but unreliable, so Unser's teammates Rick Mears and Danny Sullivan stuck with Cosworth engines. Things improved when Newman/Haas and Patrick Racing joined Penske as Ilmor-Chevy customers in 1987. From 1988 through 1991 Ilmor-Chevys won all but two races. (Dan Boyd).

Opposite: With the season under way, Bobby, Horne, and Newbury tried to make their Lola-Judd competitive with the Ilmor-Chevrolet teams. Horne believes the reason the Judd was never the equal of the Ilmor-Chevy was because its electronic engine management capabilities were limited. (Dan Boyd)

raced exclusively that year by Penske Racing. In 1987 engines were supplied to Newman-Haas for Mario Andretti and to Patrick Racing for Emerson Fittipaldi and Kevin Cogan.

Rather than selling individual engines to teams that could then maintain and rebuild their engines in any way that suited them, Ilmor and Chevrolet introduced the engine lease program to CART. For the first time, engines were supplied, serviced, and maintained by the manufacturer for a fixed annual fee, with the race teams having nothing to do with running the engines other than bolting or unbolting them from the car. During the '90s, as Ford-Cosworth, Honda, and Toyota came into Indy or Champ car racing, engine leasing became a way of life, but back in the late '80s, it was an entirely foreign method of doing business.

"As Ilmor came on stage with the Chevrolet Indy engine, they transformed the land-scape," Steve Horne explains. "One, in the way you operated and owned the engines, and two, in performance."

Bobby believed that Horne had reached an agreement with Ilmor and Chevrolet for Truesports to race Chevy engines in 1988. "At Nazareth [Pennsylvania] in September of 1987," Bobby says, "we pretty much agreed to terms with Ilmor. In fact, that was a decision Steve made that was to haunt him later on, because we were scheduled to get the Ilmor, and then he decided to go with the Judd. I won't say I argued against it, but I was certainly kind of shocked."

"We started thinking about what we were going to have to do to maintain competitive-ness on the engine front," Horne adds. "We had a lot of discussions with Ilmor, but the price, and the idea of leasing the engines, was so foreign to us. It was going to take a million dollars to get into the program.

"Barbara [Trueman] wasn't prepared to write the check to do that, so Barbara and myself went to Budweiser and had a meeting. We said these are our choices: Stay with Cosworth and start to lose competitiveness. Switch to Ilmor, which we needed Bud to help us with financially, or there was a third alternative which was a Judd, which we felt had some potential."

The Judd Indy turbo V-8 was built by John Judd in England. Judd worked for three-time World Champion Jack Brabham in the '60s and was first introduced to Honda when

The Judd V-8 turbo Indy engine was substantially cheaper than the Ilmor-Chevrolet. Like the Ilmor, it was built in England. John Judd began his career with Australian Jack Brabham in the 1960s and has built engines for most major racing series, including Formula 1. (Dan Boyd)

Brabham started racing Honda Formula Two engines back in 1964. As a result, Judd's well-established engine-building shop had a long working relationship with Honda. This was the basis for what turned out to be a fruitless hope that the Judd Indy engine program ultimately would be taken over by Honda.

"Honda had given us very mixed signals," Horne concedes, "but we nevertheless decided to get involved with Judd, which in 1988 wasn't a hindrance. We still finished third in the cham-pionship, and the engine was reasonable. We should have switched to Ilmor, but we weren't financially able to do it, as a lot of teams weren't. An Ilmor lease cost a million dollars, but a deal for Judd

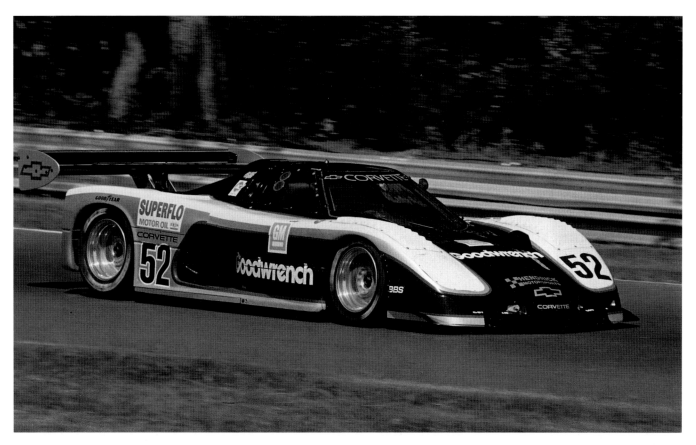

engines was half the price. My logic, which on reflection was incorrect, was that we could spend that half-million on a lot of other things. Ultimately, the downfall was that Judd didn't have the electronic capability that Ilmor had. I think that was the difference."

To Bobby's chagrin, Ilmor-Chevrolet dominated in 1988, winning all but one of the year's fifteen races. "Even with the Judd, we were in the hunt for the championship until Mid-Ohio in September," Bobby reflects. The only man to win without a Chevy that year was in fact Bobby, who scored his lone victory of the season in the Pocono 500, beating Al Unser Jr. and a depleted field. He also finished second four times, at Long Beach, Cleveland, the Michigan 500, and Elkhart Lake, and finished third in the championship behind Danny Sullivan and Al Jr.

That season Bobby also raced a Corvette GTP car for Rick Hendrick in three IMSA races.

He drove the purpose-built Corvette at West Palm Beach, Columbus, and California's Del Mar, finishing fifth at Del Mar. "I was pleased at Columbus because I was the first normally aspirated car on the grid," Bobby says. "I outqualified the Jaguars when Tom Walkinshaw had all the hotshoes driving for him."

During the summer of 1988 Bobby had reached an important decision. He would leave Truesports at the end of the season after seven years, eighteen

Above: Bobby drove the Corvette GTP run by Rick Hendrick's team in three IMSA races in 1988. The car wasn't very reliable, and his best finish was a fifth at Del Mar. That would turn out to be the last year Bobby raced a sports or GT-type car. (Hal Crocker)

Left: In the pits during the Pocono 500. Bobby had qualified on the outside of the front row beside Penske drivers Mears and Sullivan. "I almost put it on pole," Bobby says, "but I had a huge moment in turn one and almost crashed the thing." He won the race, beating Al Unser Jr. and Roberto Guerrero. (Steve Swope)

A quick pit stop in Toronto helped Bobby maintain his position. He qualified fifth and finished in the same place behind three Chevy-powered cars—driven by Al Unser Jr., Danny Sullivan, and Emerson Fittipaldi—and Michael Andretti's Cosworth-engine car. (Dan Boyd)

wins, and two championships. "By September I had announced I was going elsewhere, and I think Steve had lost interest in seeing how well we could do in the championship because we lost engines in the last several races. We lost an engine at Laguna. I was running second or third, and the engine blew up. It was kind of a disappointing end to a long relationship."

Bobby made the decision because he wanted to be paid more money and to find a way to have more control over the equipment he would be racing. In 1988, Bobby's first choice was to drive for the new Porsche team that

As the season wound down it became clear that the relationship between Bobby and Steve Horne was unraveling. Bobby was headed to Maury Kraines's team for 1989 and Horne was looking for a new driver. As Bobby puts it, "The party was over at that point." (Dan Boyd)

was being planned for 1989. "At the Cleveland race I met with [Porsche's North American racing director] Al Holbert and [Porsche's Motorsports director] Helmut Flegl, and Holbert wanted me to drive the car. He was trying to push it. But Flegl wanted a European, and they chose Fabi," Bobby says.

After the Porsche option was closed, he chose to join Maury Kraines's Kraco team for 1989. Kraines had made his fortune through founding and selling Kraco car stereos. He started his own Indy car team in 1981 and first achieved success with Michael Andretti at the wheel. He had hired Adrian Newey away from Truesports at the end of 1985, but by 1988 Newey was long gone to F1, and the younger Andretti was getting ready to join father Mario in 1989 in an expanded, two-car Newman-Haas team, which left Kraines looking for a new driver.

"By then Bobby was a top dog out there," Horne comments. "Bobby Rahal and Rick Mears were the guys, with Michael Andretti coming up. Other team owners had made a run at Bobby a couple of times, and he felt he was being underpaid, I think. So he moved on to Kraco. Maury Kraines wrote him a big check, and away he went.

"It was money, more than anything, I think," Horne continues. "Bobby wanted a Chevy, but he wanted more money." Horne believed that Bobby should have been paid what he was worth, but he was unable to offer Bobby a million dollars outright, because he had

Bobby storms over the top of the esses at Mid-Ohio. He qualified third at his home track that year but didn't make the finish. Bobby explains: "We were running strong, and Ludwig Heimrath Jr. lost it on a restart in the rain, came across into me, and took me into the guardrail." (Rich Chenet)

to run the team without any financial support from the owners. If Bobby was going to make that much, he would have to earn it through prize money. Horne had tried to enlist help from the team's sponsor, Budweiser, but was turned down.

"Fundamentally, I could understand he was worth it, but I couldn't convince Barbara Trueman or Budweiser that they should pay him," Horne says. "I was surprised more than anything at Budweiser's attitude toward it, because they'd made the investment in Bobby and the team, but they didn't stand behind us to

make it a long-term relationship. They didn't get the ultimate return, I don't think."

Horne speculates that there may have been other factors that contributed to Bobby's leaving. "Maybe some of that was because Jim was no longer around, because he was always good at managing people. I wasn't an expert at it. I learned the hard way, and perhaps I underestimated that part of the business a little bit. Maybe that frustrated Bobby a little bit, too. So he went to Maury Kraines, who said, 'Whatever you want, you're going to get.' So really, that was the end of a pretty long-standing relationship, and we ended up with [Scott] Pruett for 1989."

Horne says that despite losing Bobby, his respect never wavered for Rahal's driving ability and commitment to the sport. "Bobby was growing in stature in the community in Columbus, and building up pretty good business interests," Horne points out. "But I never thought his commitment to winning or driving changed. His commitment to other interests grew, but he was always 100 percent committed to racing.

"It's hard for me to figure out how and why our relationship worked so well," Horne reflects. "It just clicked. I think professionally we both were able to leverage each other to the maximum, and we had a really good group of people.

"The thing about Bob was that for me, he was and probably still is the most complete driver I've worked with," Horne declares. "He was extremely good, and wily out of the car. He was, as all drivers are, I think, somewhat insecure. He was trying to plan for his future

and look after number one, but as a driver I think he was always a big team player. He had great technical ability and really knew what was going on with the car."

Ten years after Horne and Bobby went their separate ways, Horne still rated Rahal very high. "In reality," Horne remarks, "I think it was surprising that we stayed together for so long. It was unique, and is still probably quite unique, for a driver to stay with a team for seven years, particularly given the turmoil we went through.

"At that stage, Truesports was a pretty big organization. We were running an Indy Lights team as well. In 1987 we won both the Indy car and the Indy Lights championships. I got a kick out of that, and I think Bobby did as well. Nobody's done that before, or since."

Bobby has equal respect for Horne and enjoys great pride in everything Truesports accomplished during his seven years with the team. "I think, to be really honest," Bobby mulls, "if you were to ask Steve and I today, 'Would you have done things differently?' we probably both would say we would have. With Steve, you never questioned his desire to win. He was a tough son of a bitch, but I guess you have to be a tough son of a bitch to win. There were some politics that I didn't appreciate at the time and still probably wouldn't appreciate, but boy, I tell you, we won a lot of races together."

"It was a kind of unholy alliance."

Bobby's new life with Maury Kraines's Kraco team came about for many reasons and was instigated largely by Kraco's manager, Barry Green. Friends since Bobby's Formula Atlantic days, Bobby and Green were golfing buddies, playing together whenever possible as their travels coincided around the country.

Green had tried to hire Bobby on a couple of occasions and had actually done so for a brief time at the end of 1981 when he was managing Paul Newman's CanAm team, for whom Bobby drove the last four CanAm races. After Newman closed the doors on his CanAm team in 1982 to become partners with Carl Haas in CART, Green also moved into Indy car racing. He joined Gerald Forsythe's new team with Teo Fabi driving, and in 1983 the little Italian was CART's rookie of the year, winning four races and finishing second to Al Unser Sr. in the championship.

Their success was turned upside down the following year, however, as Fabi lost interest in Indy cars and left the team midseason to try to break into Formula One. Forsythe hired various drivers to replace Fabi, but after losing sponsor Skoal at the end of the year, the Chicago-based industrialist decided to pull out of racing, although ten years later he would return, initially in partnership with Green, then on his own.

Opposite: Bobby and the Kraco team confer with Al Unser Jr. on setup strategy at Indianapolis. Working with a teammate and sharing technical information were new experiences for both drivers. Neither was completely comfortable with the situation, but both made the best of it during 1990 and 1991. (Jori Potiker)

Above: Bobby and new boss Maury Kraines announce their partnership for 1989. Kraines paid Bobby a salary of $1 million for the year to drive his Cosworth-powered Lola. Bobby knew the engines would be stretched to the maximum but hoped to arrange a deal for Ilmor-Chevys the following year. (Dan Boyd)

165

Following Forsythe's pullout, Green moved to Maury Kraines's team, where Michael Andretti was the lead driver. Michael had started his Indy car career with the Kraco team at the end of 1983, and with Green on board as team manager in 1986 and 1987. Young Andretti won seven races and finished second both years to Bobby in CART's PPG Cup championship. Like Bobby, Andretti found himself outpowered in 1988 by the new Ilmor-Chevy Indy V-8. Michael didn't win a race in 1988 and by midseason had decided to join his father, Mario, for 1989 in an expanded two-car Newman-Haas team powered by Chevrolet engines.

That left Maury Kraines with the will and the money to pay a top driver to replace the hard-charging Andretti. The timing and money, combined with Kraines's get-it-done personality and Green's encouraging presence, soon convinced Bobby that Kraco was the way to go.

"I'd known Barry for a long time, and at one point in, I think 1985, he tried to get me to drive for Forsythe," Bobby says. "But things were going so well with Truesports at the time that I just didn't see any point in doing that. But by the end of 1988, Barry was at Kraco and Maury Kraines was looking for a driver and prepared to pay what I considered my fair market value, something I couldn't get at Truesports."

The downside at Kraco was that the team was still running outdated Cosworth DFX engines, which meant Bobby was not only outpowered but also failed to finish quite a few races as Kraco's engine-building shop stretched the old engine beyond its maximum in an attempt to match the Ilmor-Chevrolet. Bobby hit trouble in four of the year's first five races, and that set the tone for the rest of the year.

"It was neat to say you made a million dollars, but the thing was, I'd made more than that from 1985 through 1988 at Truesports just because of performance. There was no question that about halfway through the year, I was very disappointed.

"At Indy that year we qualified inside the third row, but we knew the thing was blowing plugs out. It had really small spark plugs in it, and if it wasn't blowing the plugs out, it was throwing rod bearings or dropping valves. Going into that year's Indy 500, I would have guaranteed you we weren't going to finish, and sure enough, thirty laps into the race, we were gone."

Things picked up a little in the middle of the year as Bobby finished second at Portland in June and was third at Cleveland. Then, at the Meadowlands in July, Bobby drove brilliantly to score his lone win of the year.

In Toronto, Bobby qualified fourth and led Mario Andretti's Chevy-powered Lola in the race, but inevitably, he didn't make the finish. Engine problems brought his run to an early end. (Dan Boyd)

Bobby rates his victory at the Meadowlands in changeable wet-dry conditions as one of the ten best drives of his career. He is joined on the victory podium by Emerson Fittipaldi and Scott Pruett. This would be Bobby's lone win of 1989. (Art Flores)

"The only highlight of '89 was winning at the Meadowlands in the rain, which is the great equalizer," Bobby comments. "I list that as one of my ten best drives. To be honest, I can't remember too much about that season prior to or after that, because none of it was very good."

Indeed, the Meadowlands was by far the high point of 1989, as Bobby finished barely more than half the races. He was sixth in the Pocono 500 and took seventh and sixth, respectively, at Nazareth and Laguna Seca at the end of the year to finish ninth in the championship.

"We actually had a fabulous year in terms of performance against the odds," Green says. "Bobby drove so well with a Cosworth against the Chevys. We were definitely down on power. We were severely handicapped, and I think he raised his level to try and compete. Bobby qualified well and just drove the wheels off the car. In a way, it was probably a very good season for him."

During 1989, Bobby began to develop a pivotal relationship with the Honda Motor Company. For one thing, he opened the first of his three automobile dealerships in January 1989, a Honda dealership in Mechanicsburg, Pennsylvania. He was also able to attract an emissary from Honda, Michihiro Asaka, to be his guest at the Long Beach CART race in

April 1989. Bobby began to persistently encouraged the Japanese manufacturer to think about going Indy car racing.

Asaka had no racing experience. He was a noise and vibration engineer for Honda, but ultimately he would become Honda's Indy car project chief and work with American Honda's executive vice president, Tom Elliott, who took charge of managing all aspects of Honda's CART engine program once it got under way in 1993. As the Honda project slowly gathered momentum, it became key to Bobby's future plans.

Bobby's pursuit of Honda moved slowly over the next three years. After Asaka's visit to Long Beach in the spring of 1989, Bobby followed up with a discreet visit of his own to Honda's research and development test center and track at Tochigi, where he discussed racing and Indy cars, and was offered a test run in one of the prototype NSX high-performance sports cars. He competed that year at the Macau GP in a "superstars of racing" celebrity race for which top drivers from all forms of racing were brought in to drive a fleet of Mazda RX-7s on a street circuit in the freewheeling southeast-Asian city.

"After my first meeting with Mr. Asaka in Long Beach, and in the years that followed, 1989, '90 and '91, there were phone calls back and forth. Then Mr. Asaka had a brain aneurysm. It damn near killed him. He just disappeared off the radar screen.

"I had gotten to know him and liked him personally. He had been in L.A. for a while at Honda R&D in Torrance, and he got transferred back to Japan, and that's when it happened. Debi and I were just sick when we heard about it. Everything just kind of stopped, you know, because he was our friend and our conduit to Honda, and I'll never forget, Debi and I were in bed watching TV one night around ten or eleven o'clock, and the phone rang, and it was Mr. Asaka!"

Bobby and Debi drink a toast with Michihiro Asaka in Honda's corporate suite at the Phoenix Grand Prix Formula One race in 1990. Asaka was Honda's emissary in observing and studying Indy car racing with a view to competing in the CART series. (Rahal collection)

Bobby had not heard from him in six or eight months. "I told him I heard he damn near died," Bobby continues. "I remember I had tears in my eyes, I was so happy to hear him talk, and know he was OK. And then, after a period of time, we got back on track with the program."

In 1990, Asaka and two other engineers from Honda R&D visited Indianapolis where Bobby finished second. Near the end of the following year, two other Honda R&D engineers, closely allied with Honda's president, Nobuhiko Kawamoto, flew to Elkhart Lake, a race where Bobby qualified on the pole and finished fourth.

"It was kind of funny because we were always buying them tickets," Bobby recalls. "They didn't want to hang around the pits. They wanted to be unobtrusive—they wanted to observe—so they were in the grandstands, way on the other side of the pit area, observing."

Without making a conscious decision about it, Bobby stopped racing sports and GTP cars during this time. "I don't know if I lost interest or felt I was doing enough as it was. In January of '89, we opened the Honda dealership, and I guess I felt I just had enough on my plate. Also, the independents like Bob Akin and Bruce Leven and Rob Dyson who ran good cars had gone by then. The factory Nissan and Jaguar teams were dominating IMSA.

"I pursued halfheartedly driving a Jaguar. I met with Tom Walkinshaw, and there was some interest in doing Le Mans, but it never came to anything. I also had an offer to drive a Sauber at Le Mans with Jochen Mass, but more than anything, I just felt like I had enough going on."

By the end of 1989, it was obvious there was no point in flogging on any longer in CART with a Cosworth or any engine other than an Ilmor-Chevy. Bobby made the point quite clearly to Maury Kraines, who had heard the same complaint the year before from Michael Andretti. The problem was, Ilmor and Chevrolet would supply only a limited number of teams with engines and claimed they had no more capacity. But Kraines kept trying to find a way and pulled it off by proposing a merger with Rick Galles's team.

Galles had Chevrolet engines with Al Unser Jr. driving. His team was based in Albuquerque, New Mexico, home to both the Galles and Unser families, and Al Jr., had spent most of his professional racing career with Galles's team. The agreement Kraines struck with Galles was that the Kraco team would close its shop in Compton, California, and move to Albuquerque, where any of Kraines's employees who chose to make the move would be absorbed into a combined and expanded two-car Galles-Kraco operation. Green took over as team manager, with many of his people deciding to uproot and move from California to New Mexico.

Near the end of 1989, Bobby opened the first of his three automobile dealerships, a Honda agency in Mechanicsburg, Pennsylvania. Bobby had met people in Honda's advertising agency through a friend of Mike's. He also got to know Shoichiro Irimajiri, who ran Honda of America manufacturing in Marysville, Ohio, and lived in Columbus. These key relationships helped Bobby establish his franchise. (Rahal collection)

"I had to hand it to Maury," Bobby says. "He did that deal with Rick Galles, and I couldn't think of two more unlikely people to be partners. But Maury wanted to win, and that was Maury's only way to get the Ilmor."

The leasing program and limited supply introduced to CART by Ilmor and Chevrolet created a lot of debate and ill feeling, sowing some of the seeds for the Indy Racing League's breakaway from CART seven years later. Al Unser Sr. tried and was unable to race at Indianapolis for Vince Granatelli in 1991 because he and Granatelli were told no Chevrolet engines were available. The decision enraged both Unser and Indianapolis Motor Speedway president, Tony George, who attempted without success to mediate on Unser's behalf.

"If I see any reason why the IRL was started from an engine standpoint," Bobby reflects, "it was the way Ilmor lorded over who got engines and who didn't, particularly at Indy with Al Sr. in 1991. I think it was wrong, and, probably rightly so, it created problems for CART down the road."

Nevertheless, Bobby at last had a Chevrolet engine behind him, and he and new team-mate Unser were very competitive in 1990 and 1991. "The Galles-Kraco years were great," Green comments. "The team itself didn't jell as well as it should have, but we still worked well together. I can still see the great benefits of having two great drivers, Bobby and Al, working together. And Bobby brought a heck of a lot to the party.

"I don't think they were ever the best of friends—they're two very different people—but they both understood that they could use each other, and that's the name of the game in a two-car team."

Bobby says he enjoyed his two years with Galles-Kraco despite a palpable separation within the team. "It was a difficult situation because one half was the Galles group and one half was the Kraco group," Bobby points out. "Barry was running the show, but guys like [Al Jr.'s crew chief] Owen Snyder had been with Galles forever, and there was definitely a schism between the two organizations. Even though it was all one team, you were never

Both Bobby and Barry Green believe they lost the 1990 Indianapolis 500 by being too conservative on the final pit stop. Bobby's car understeered in the closing stages, which was complicated by a broken wing adjuster. In hindsight Green feels they should have risked a larger adjustment to help Bobby keep Luyendyk at bay. (Art Flores)

Bobby leads Mario Andretti and a midpack group at Elkhart Lake in 1990. He qualified and finished seventh, not one of his best showings at Road America. (Rich Chenet)

together. If I beat Al on a given day, all the Galles guys were pissed off and the Kraco guys were happy, and vice versa.

"It was kind of an unholy alliance. It was a marriage of convenience and yet out of that, there was a very healthy sense of competition between Al and I, although I swear Al was never straightforward with the technical information he was giving me. I'm sure he feels the same about me, although I can tell you I was! I guess if I ever felt a problem with Galles-Kraco, it was the team's definite bent towards Al, being Albuquerque-based."

Bobby finished second to Rick Mears in the 1990 season opener at Phoenix, beating new teammate Al Jr., who was third. At Long Beach, Bobby failed to finish as Unser took the first of six races he would win on the way to that year's championship. At Indianapolis, Bobby qualified fourth and battled for the lead most of the way with Emerson Fittipaldi. In the end, however, he finished a very disappointed second to Arie Luyendyk.

Green says that the best race he had working with Bobby was probably 1990 at Indy when Bobby finished second. "He drove a tremendous race, and I felt we let him down a little bit because from the pits, it's our job to manage the race and to keep an eye on everyone that's behind. We found ourselves leading strongly in the middle of the race, and we ran nice and conservatively at that point, and I never really saw Luyendyk coming.

"I think we were a little too conservative on the last stop. We knew we needed to make some adjustments for some understeer, but we were just a little too conservative because we were running so well in the middle of the race. I didn't see Luyendyk coming, and I thought we had the field covered, so I possibly let the side down. But Bobby drove a tremendous race, and while it was still great to finish second at Indy, it was a big blow in the stomach, because we really allowed ourselves to get beaten."

Bobby was second also at Cleveland and finished behind teammate Unser in a Galles-Kraco one-two in the Michigan 500. He finished third in Denver and at Nazareth, taking fourth in the championship behind teammate Al Jr., Michael Andretti, and Mears.

Opposite: Al Unser Jr. and Bobby recount their race after finishing one-two in the Marlboro 500 at Michigan, while co-team owners Kraines and Galles share the glory. Though the two co-owners had very different personalities and led a team that was somewhat divided, they got along comfortably. (Dan Boyd)

Following pages: Bobby clips an apex en route to a second-place finish to Emerson Fittipaldi in Detroit. Unlike road courses, a temporary street circuit has no runoff area. "They're the ultimate challenge, because you have to use every inch possible, and you only have a finite number of inches available," Bobby says. (Michael C. Brown)

The following season, Bobby had an even better year, taking second to Michael Andretti in the championship, with Al Jr. third. Bobby was second in the first three races of 1991, Surfers Paradise, Australia; Long Beach; and Phoenix. At Long Beach, the team took another one-two as Unser won the California street race for the fourth consecutive year. At Indianapolis, Bobby again qualified fourth and ran with the leaders before blowing an engine after 130 laps.

In the second half of the season, Bobby was on the podium seven times, including for another win at the Meadowlands, his third at the temporary New Jersey track-in-a-parking lot, this time in sunny, dry weather. Bobby was still in the championship hunt going into the season closer at Laguna Seca but failed to finish. His engine blew as championship rival Andretti won the race from the pole and took his first PPG Cup title. After climbing out of his expired car, Bobby walked down to Andretti's pit and congratulated each Newman-Haas crewman.

"I think one of the defining moments for me, as far as the gentleman Bobby is," comments Debi, "was when Bobby got out of the car after he dropped out of the race at Laguna and went over and shook hands with Michael's team. To me that said a lot about

Bobby leads Al Jr. in the 1990 street race in downtown Denver. His car's air jack failed, and Bobby had to run the last half of the race on one set of tires. Unser eventually won, with Bobby finishing third behind Danny Sullivan. (Michael C. Brown)

Bobby's character and the person he is, and I was very proud of him for that. I take a lot of those memories away from racing, his demeanor in difficult times."

Team manager Green offers his assessment of Bobby from those days. "I don't think Bobby was blazingly fast for any one or two laps, but he was very, very consistent," Green says. "Come race day, as long as he was reasonably happy with his car, he was going to do those laps, every time. He wasn't a guy that would put together that one big qualifying lap, but you knew that whatever speed you qualified at, you were pretty comfortable racing at. I think that was his strength."

Bobby says his two years with Al Jr. prove that having two number-one drivers who are properly managed and have equal status is key to success in racing. "The end result was that Al and I pushed each other to the point that in 1990 and '91, the Galles-Kraco team was the dominant team," Bobby recounts. "I think we had three or four one-twos. Al won more races than I did, certainly, but in 1990, I finished fourth in the championship, and in 1991, I was second. Al won in 1990, and I think he was third or fourth in 1991. It speaks well for people who argue that you want two number ones pushing each other, because the result just raises everybody's game."

Al Jr. shares Bobby's view of that era. "The Galles-Kraco years were very good for me," Unser says. "I won my first championship with Bobby Rahal as my teammate. As the Galles team, we were not experienced in how team operations and management worked between two cars, especially with two number-one drivers." Al agrees that there were definitely two distinct teams, but felt that's the way Rick Galles wanted it. Galles had the two teams compete against each other in pit stop contests and incentives.

"But it definitely worked for me," Al Jr. continues, "because having two number-one drivers and two number-one crews brought the level up. My whole crew from those years went on to become crew chiefs. I learned an awful lot on how teammates should get along, because I got along with Bobby very well. We did have our differences, but definitely at the next race all was forgotten, and we would go on down the road. That was the beginning for me of working with a teammate, and I don't like teammates. I never have and I never will. But I had to get along with them for the benefit of the team, not just myself."

For many observers, the most amazing thing about the Galles-Kraco years was that two characters as dissimilar as Galles and Kraines could work together so effectively. Galles came from a well-established family of Albuquerque automobile dealers, while Kraines was an entirely self-made man in the car stereo and electronic gadget business.

"I enjoyed my time with Rick and Maury," Bobby says. "They were very different. Maury was a tough son of a bitch. When it came time to negotiate, you didn't negotiate. You basically said yes to what he was going to offer. But Maury was a tough guy. He grew up the hard way, and he made it his way.

"You could make a movie about Maury's story, and Rick was totally the opposite. Rick was from a successful family, and that's not being disparaging to Rick. That's just reality. Rick came from a different background, and that's why they were highly unusual partners, and yet they worked together very well for some time."

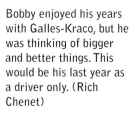

Bobby enjoyed his years with Galles-Kraco, but he was thinking of bigger and better things. This would be his last year as a driver only. (Rich Chenet)

While he was with Kraines and Galles, Bobby also became a fitness fanatic, working out regularly in the gym and riding bicycles. These days, when he's at home, Bobby and Debi work out together. "I started in about 1990 really starting to work out, and it's been for the better ever since," Bobby declares. "As a driver, it just gave me far more stamina. I had more energy, more strength, and more staying power.

"My physical fitness is something that I take a great deal of pride in and am committed to because I want the remainder of my life to be active, to be able to do things, to go skiing or hiking or go scuba diving with my kids. I want to be somebody who can participate with his children as they grow up, not to be sitting there watching from the sidelines. And the only way you're going to do that is to take care of yourself. It's not easy, but it's necessary if you expect to live this way."

Celebrating another one-two with teammate Al Jr. at the Meadowlands; third-place driver Rick Mears is in the background. This was Bobby's third win in five years at the Meadowlands. It was also the last CART race held at the New Jersey sporting facility. (Steve Swope)

"I thought you'd never ask."

During his time with Galles-Kraco, Bobby was always on the lookout for something different. For one thing, he used to talk in those days about wanting to have control over his own destiny. That meant having a major personal sponsor, if not owning his own team. For another, he was continuing to work away quietly and persistently at convincing Honda to go Indy car racing.

In the middle of 1991, Bobby started talking to Pat Patrick through Patrick's marketing man, Bruce Barnes, about driving for the Michigan oilman's team the following year. Patrick had owned an Indy car team for twenty-five years and in 1978 co-founded CART with Roger Penske. Patrick sold his original team to Chip Ganassi in 1989 but came back almost immediately to form a new team to campaign Alfa Romeo's ex-Ferrari engines. Lavishly bankrolled but seriously underpowered, the Alfa engine program went nowhere, and by the summer of 1991, it was facing the ax.

Patrick had sponsorship from Miller Brewing but needed engines and a driver if he was to stay in business. On the engine front, Patrick was in trouble because Ilmor's Mario Ilien and Paul Morgan would not do business with him after he shipped one of his Ilmor-Chevys to Alfa

Above: Side by side with former teammate Al Unser Jr. on the high banks of the 2-mile Michigan superspeedway. Al Jr. drives the unique Galmer chassis, with which he won that year's Indy 500. Bobby's engine failed, and he didn't finish the race. Unser placed fourth. (Dan Boyd)

Opposite: Bobby and Carl Hogan brandish their PPG Cups in victory lane at Laguna. "For me, it was the best of my three championships," Bobby says. "I was an owner-driver, and I had taken many risks, both business risks, as with Miller, and personal risks, like pulling Jimmy Prescott from Galles and asking him and his family to move again for me. There was a lot on the line." (Art Flores)

Right: Ilmor partner and chief designer Mario Ilien was adamant that his company would not supply Pat Patrick with engines, because Patrick had shipped an Ilmor engine to Alfa Romeo for Alfa to reverse-engineer. But he was happy to make an agreement with Bobby for the 1992 season. (Art Flores)

Opposite: At the opening race of the 1992 season, Surfers Paradise, Bobby finished third behind winner Emerson Fittipaldi and Rick Mears. Here Bobby leads Mears, John Andretti, and Fabrizzio Barbazza. (Michael C. Brown)

Romeo back in 1989. Alfa Romeo took the engine apart, inspected it, and ran it on an Alfa Romeo dynamometer in a failed effort to learn Ilmor's secrets, an episode that deeply infuriated Ilien and Morgan.

"I did it for a couple of reasons," Bobby says about his planned move to Patrick's team for 1992. "One, I wanted to be involved with Miller. Two, I'd been working on this Honda project for some time, and I sensed there was the possibility, not a sure thing, that it was going to happen, and I wanted to make sure I was in a situation where I could take advantage of that.

"I tried to get a one-year deal with Galles-Kraco, but they wanted a three-year deal or nothing, and I didn't want to do that," Bobby explains. "And Patrick and Miller were willing to sign what was in effect three one-year deals, which gave me the ability to make a change if I wanted to. Of course, I understood how important it was to a driver's career to have a sponsor like Miller. Miller merchandised with their racing program and advertised that they were in racing, and that they were in it with you. I hadn't had that since Budweiser. No offense to Kraco, but Kraco did very little marketing through the racing program.

"So I began talking to Pat somewhere around June or July of 1991. Bruce Barnes was the go-between. I knew what I wanted to do in 1993, which was have my own team, and I had been talking to Carl Hogan. Our whole plan was that we would start Rahal-Hogan in 1993.

"Well, the thing fell apart in that Pat couldn't get an engine and Miller wasn't going to approve something other than a Chevy. They had been through the wilderness with the Alfa

In the second race, Bobby scored a dominant win at Phoenix. He led all the way, and here leads Michael Andretti. Eddie Cheever and Emerson Fittipaldi finished second and third. The win brought elation and relief to his sponsor, Miller, which had been conspicuously absent from the podium during their failed Alfa Romeo experience. (Michael C. Brown)

At Toronto, Bobby qualified on the pole and ran one-two with Michael Andretti for most of the day. On the last stop, Bobby beat Michael out of the pits but Michael made a daring pass and took the lead. Bobby had to stop for fuel again but still finished second behind Michael. (Michael C. Brown)

project, so they were flexing their muscle a little bit, for which you couldn't blame them.

"Events started to speed up to the point that I went to Carl and I said, 'Well, Carl, what do you think about next year, 1992?' And he said, 'I thought you'd never ask.' I think that's a direct quote. So I went to the Miller people and said, 'There's this possibility. Would you think about it?' And therein lay the seeds that started Rahal-Hogan."

Carl Hogan owns a very successful truck leasing business based in St. Louis. He ran a top Formula 5000 team in the '70s and a CanAm operation in the '80s. After pulling out of the fading CanAm series, Hogan's interest in racing continued, and he returned to the sport at the end of 1991 as Bobby's partner.

"I had been following the series a little with Chip Ganassi for 1990 and 1991," says Hogan, who had leased a tractor-trailer to Ganassi's team. "I really had no intention of ever getting back into racing. And then in 1991, Bobby came to me at Elkhart Lake and said would I be interested in possibly forming a partnership with him and getting back in racing, and I said, 'Well, yeah, we'll talk about it.'" Hogan had been approached by another team, but he and Bobby continued their discussions, and when the season was over, Bobby met with Hogan in Florida. Together the two of them assembled a package, including budgets and sponsorship needs, for the team.

"I think Bobby was very pleased when I said, 'Yes, let's do it.' Because I said, 'What would you do for a year?' He was under contract and couldn't do anything else, and I was ready to get going and do it. We took a look at everything, including the wind tunnel operation Patrick had in England. It was a busy time, but we got it done real quick."

Bobby agrees those were a hectic few months. "It was a very busy time because I was flying all over the place, trying to put all this stuff together," he recalls. "I had agreed to go with Pat at Vancouver in 1991. Prior to Elkhart, which was in late September that year, I met with Dick Strup, who was the head of marketing at Miller, and it was at that point that the association and our friendship was renewed."

Strup and Bobby discussed the goals they both had for their racing program, and at the end of the year, when it became clear that Patrick couldn't get the Ilmor, their deal came together quickly.

"In Pat's defense, and to Pat's credit," Bobby says, "the guy was an unbelievable gentleman. In purchasing the assets of his team, the guy was totally forthright and up front. There was no bullshit, and it frankly kind of countered every bad thing I'd ever heard."

The partnership with Hogan was shared fifty-fifty. "Carl's participation essentially bought equipment, or capital goods," Bobby explains. "None of Carl's money was used in the operating budget. The sponsors—Miller, Total originally, and then Shell—paid the operating budget."

The new Rahal-Hogan team discuss technical issues in the pits. From left to right: Carl Hogan, Bobby, engineer Steve Newey, team manager Jim McGee; Jimmy Prescott is in the foreground. Bobby credits veteran manager McGee as one of the keys to his winning that year's PPG Cup title. (Dan Boyd)

With Patrick out of the picture, the way was clear for Bobby and Hogan to wrap up an agreement with Ilmor for engines. On the chassis front, Patrick had been a valued Lola customer, while Bobby had raced Lolas for five consecutive years and was entirely happy to continue with Lola. Bobby also brought his personal chief mechanic, Jimmy Prescott, with him from Galles-Kraco, but the rest of the former Patrick team continued almost unchanged from 1991, operating out of the same rented shop in Indianapolis.

"I have to say to some degree it was an advantage having the team in Indianapolis and me in Columbus," Bobby says about Rahal-Hogan's first year. "Carl did a lot of the grunt work, along with [team managers] Scott Roembke and Jim McGee and the rest of what had been Patrick Racing. Even though I was a part-owner, I ended up being treated in a lot of respects like a driver, and I don't doubt for a minute that there was some benefit to that.

"But the big thing was, it was a great organization. With only one car, we weren't a big team, but the people we had were smart and tough. They knew what needed to be done, and from the first day we tested to the last race, there was no question that all the ingredients were in place."

Bobby started the year with a good second place behind Emerson Fittipaldi at the season-opening street race in Surfers Paradise, Australia. At round two on the 1-mile Phoenix oval a few weeks later, he qualified second and dominated the race, leading all the way. It was a decisive victory that sent a clear signal that as an owner-driver, Bobby was as serious a championship threat as ever. Bobby recalls that evening's deliriously happy victory celebration with people from Miller who hadn't come close to winning in three years.

Before the second-to-last race of 1992 at Nazareth, Bobby poses with Michael Andretti, Al Unser Jr., and Emerson Fittipaldi, his three remaining rivals for the PPG Cup. (Art Flores)

"Kevin Wulff from Miller had suffered through the Alfa days, and he was as happy and drunk as anyone after we won Phoenix at the beginning of the year. I'm not sure he was really ready to buy into this deal. I think Dick Strup and Miller said, 'We're going to do this.' So Kevin went to Phoenix with all his fingers crossed, and for us to win that race was like being hit by a bolt of lightning."

He was second at Long Beach the next weekend and established himself in the lead of the championship. Bobby also ran well at Indianapolis, starting quietly from the fourth row but moving quickly into the hunt until a cut tire gave him a scary moment and cost him a lap in the pits. He wound up finishing sixth, running as fast as the leaders all the way, and left the Speedway still on top in points. Bobby followed up with an excellent win in Detroit. At Milwaukee, he won the pole but finished second to Michael Andretti.

"It just went from strength to strength," Bobby remarks. "We had a lot of good races. We won every short oval with the exception of Milwaukee. We were on the pole and finished second at Milwaukee and should have won except for a foul-up on tire pressures at the first stop, which killed us."

Bobby scored his third win of the year from the pole in the inaugural CART race at the new 1-mile New Hampshire Speedway and again took the pole position in the streets of

Toronto a few weeks later, but finished second to Michael once more. He failed to finish the Michigan 500, as did most of the front-runners that year, championship rival Andretti included. Bobby crashed at Mid-Ohio, which was the third from the last race that year. This gave Andretti a chance to catch him in the points.

Hogan says, "We had gotten into a little bit of a slump that year at Mid-Ohio. Bobby went off the road in turn one and very truthfully, I felt he had lost a little focus because he was running his golf tournament at the same time, the day after the race at Mid-Ohio. It was a charity thing, and he wanted to do a good job, and he was working with that. After he crashed, we sat down, and I said to Bobby, 'Look, you've got to forget all this other stuff right now and get back to racing.' And I was very pleased that he responded."

At the next race, Nazareth, the Andrettis' home track, Bobby beat Michael to the checkered flag after a fierce battle and put himself in position to take the title. Hogan called some sharp pit strategy by not making a last-minute fuel stop, which was key to winning that day.

"At Nazareth we took the car out of the trailer, and Bobby was fast all weekend," Hogan says happily. "I think winning that race was the turning point. It was a little bit of a gamble, but it worked out. When they work out, you're a hero, and when they don't, you're a bum. But it worked out well that day."

To steal the championship, Andretti had to win with Bobby sixth or worse in the final race at Laguna Seca. In fact, Michael did all he could by winning from the pole, but Bobby finished a steady third, beating Michael to the championship by just four points, to win his third CART title.

Hogan is proud of his role in winning that year's PPG Cup with Bobby. "Our deal was

The pressure was enormous at Laguna Seca because the points battle was so close between Bobby and Michael Andretti. "I couldn't make any mistakes," Bobby says. "There were a lot of cars behind me, and with one little slip-up I could've lost a lot of positions, and with them the championship." He finished third and won by four points. (Dan Boyd)

that Bobby and I would share in the decision-making and running everything," Hogan explains, "but when the race weekend came, he would be a driver and I would make any decisions that were involved with the team. We stuck with that, and I think it worked out very well. I think we had a good relationship on how it worked and who did what. Bobby did a lot of the technical work, and I did a lot of the organizational work.

"As I look back," Hogan says, smiling, "I don't think we realized how good it was because we were good right off the bat. Bobby was motivated, we had a good sponsor in Miller and a reasonable budget, and we could really concentrate. We really worked hard and put a lot of emotion into it, but like anything, when you're doing it, you don't realize it. You look back and say, 'Boy, there were a lot of things that came together.'"

Bobby also remains fiercely proud of his third championship and still believes he should have prevailed in more races that year. "We should have won five races," Bobby declares.

Back at the shop, the Rahal-Hogan race-day crew members present Bobby with a small trophy of their own in appreciation for his efforts both in and out of the cockpit. (Rahal collection)

"We should have won in Milwaukee. We should have won the Marlboro Challenge at Nazareth. We dominated Nazareth the whole weekend and should have won that race on Saturday, as well as the PPG Cup race on Sunday. But we won the championship. Again, the fact that it was our first year—nobody said you could do that—but we won four races and were in a position to win more."

Indeed, Bobby's third PPG Cup title meant he was the first and only owner-driver to win a CART championship. The last man in Indy or Champ car history to win a championship prior to Bobby was A. J. Foyt, who was USAC champion as an owner-driver in 1964, 1967, 1975, and 1979. In today's world of big teams, high technology, and ever-climbing costs, it's doubtful the feat will ever again be accomplished.

"We had a great season," Bobby concludes. "It was an affirmation of everything we had spoken about that we could do, given the opportunity. A lot of people ask what was the most rewarding thing in your career, and as much as 1986 and '87 were rewarding, I think 1992 was the most rewarding because it was totally contrary, or in the face of what people expected—what people said you could or couldn't do. It was very special."

"It became almost like a black hole."

Toward the end of their championship-winning 1992 season, Bobby and Hogan made a fateful decision to take over the ailing Truesports car-building project. The decision included a move from the team's rented shop in Indianapolis to Truesports's larger, more complete shop in Hilliard, Ohio, close to Bobby's home.

For some time Steve Horne had believed the only way he could compete with teams like Penske and Newman-Haas was to build his own car, and despite a tight budget, he plunged ahead with the plan in the years immediately after Bobby left Truesports. Don Halliday, an experienced Indy car and F1 engineer and car builder, was hired to design what would be called the Truesports Indy car. The team developed an abandoned U.S. Air Force wind tunnel on the outskirts of the Columbus airport in partnership with Ohio State University.

The resulting car was small and sleek, and Scott Pruett had driven it to many good results, more often than not qualifying in the top ten in both 1991 and 1992. The team persevered with Judd engines through 1991, finally switching to Ilmor-Chevys in 1992, but by then the

Above: In January of 1993, Bobby's team poses with the RH01 in the Hilliard, Ohio, shop formerly occupied by Truesports. At this point, hopes were high, but a series of shortcomings would be discovered over the next few months. Designer Don Halliday is third from the left in the front row beside Jim Prescott and Larry "Ramjet" Randlett. (Gary Gold)

Opposite: In the pits at Indianapolis, Don Halliday, Bobby, and the team's engineers pore over reams of data in an unsuccessful attempt to figure out how to solve the RH01's problems. Neither Bobby nor teammate Mike Groff made the race. (Michael C. Brown)

energy, sponsorship, and commitment had run out. At the end of 1992, following a series of disagreements with Barbara Trueman, Horne quit the team he had run for ten years.

"About two-thirds of the way through 1992, Barbara Trueman called me up one day," Bobby says. "Barbara and I had kind of a falling-out after 1988. Prior to 1988, Barbara and I had been very close because of Jim, and I had known Barbara for fifteen or sixteen years, but after I left Truesports, we didn't see much of each other. Then, totally out of the blue, she called me and asked if I wanted to drive for her again. Well, that came as a bit of shock. I had to hand it to her for having the chutzpah to make the call. She was thinking, as they say, 'outside the box.' "

Bobby was not interested in rejoining Truesports or doing business again with Steve Horne. His displeasure with Horne's decision to spurn Ilmor-Chevrolet to commit instead to racing Judd engines in 1988 made for an uncomfortable relationship. "Steve and I were not on the best of terms, and I said there was no way I would drive for her if Steve was there," Bobby says. "Barbara said she was confident she could make the difference and create some kind of compromise, but I felt it was him or me, in effect, because 1988 had been a bad year for me.

"So I said, 'Well thanks, but I don't see how this could work, but I appreciate your interest.' And I asked if she had the budget for it, and she said, 'Well no, not right now, but....' "

Bobby says it then became clear to him that Barbara Trueman wanted to sell her late husband's race team, and wanted to assess whether they were making progress with their car.

Bobby confers with Carl Hogan at Phoenix where he qualified seventh but had a horrific race. The RH01's handling deteriorated, becoming erratic and unpredictable, and Bobby withdrew. Mario Andretti won the race, with Raul Boesel second, and Jimmy Vasser third. (Michael C. Brown)

Bobby agreed to test the car, and if things went well, he would take over the project. "We went off and did a test, and I felt the car had some promise. We were so confident in the team's abilities, we thought we could turn a sow's ear into silk purse. And the fact that the shop was in Ohio, and because of my relationship with Jim, it was kind of a dream to take over this facility."

Bobby believed there were solid practical reasons for moving his team to Truesports besides an obvious emotional bond. Many teams were based in Indianapolis and, inevitably, there was a lot of interaction between them. This made it difficult to keep secrets and easy for employees to be disloyal because they could

easily move from one team to another. There were financial issues involved, too, and Ohio-based Red Roof Inns was going to be a sponsor.

Hogan agreed with and approved of Bobby's thinking. "Penske built his own car, and Carl Haas was the factory guy for Lola, and we felt we weren't going to get anything until Newman-Haas was one year ahead of us," Hogan comments. "And of course, March was out of business by then. The timing was such that the Truesports thing was dissolving or liquidating. So Bobby said he wanted to take a crack at it. I said, 'Well, how good do you think it will be?' He said he thought that if we could just get a good car, we could make it better."

Steve Horne believes Bobby made an emotional rather than a business decision in taking over the project. "When I left Truesports," Horne says, "it was really because I was told after Indy to cut the budget in half for the rest of the season, and I couldn't figure out how to do that without decimating the team. So I decided I didn't want to do it anymore. It was not a logical thing to do. So I left, and at the end of '92, Bobby was sold a bill of goods, to be honest.

"I think it was the wrong thing to do," Horne continues, "because all the momentum, all the steam, had been taken out of it in the middle of the season. All the development, all the ideas and thoughts that should have happened to make that car continue to rise up the competitive ladder, had gone the other way. He bought it on emotion rather than logic."

Horne appears to have been right. With all the best intentions, and a huge effort from the team, the renamed Rahal-Hogan RH01 project failed. "Unfortunately, it was a disaster,"

Bobby gets down to work in his office that overlooks the shop floor in Hilliard. Moving into the former Truesports shop just a few miles from his home in nearby Dublin was the culmination of a dream. This is still Bobby's office today. (Gary Gold)

Bobby's race at Cleveland did not last long. "I had made a hell of a start," Bobby says. "It looked like the Charge of the Light Brigade. I'd gone from fifteenth on the grid to sixth, and I got hit twice from behind. Once by Luyendyk and once by Mark Smith, who spun me. Then Guerrero hit me, and that was that." (Art Flores)

Bobby shakes his head. "Carl and I spent a great deal of time sitting down with various people, including Don Halliday; my chief mechanic, Jim Prescott; and our team manager, Tim Cindric—really everybody that we respected—for their input." Based on their conferences, and on information from Halliday about the standard of the equipment they were buying and the design directions, they decided to go ahead with the project.

Their original plan was to race the existing car while they designed and built a new car. "But the reality was, we spent so much time refurbishing and replacing the spares we thought were good that we never had the time to really create something new," Bobby says. "So it was behind right from the word go, and as a result, there was no way we were going to be running a new car in 1993. We were going to be running a hashed-over 1991 car.

"The way it unfolded was that the equipment we got wasn't in the condition that it was purported to be. Much of the equipment needed to be totally replaced or rebuilt." They had planned to begin work immediately on a fresh design but wound up spending their time simply getting the old cars ready to race, which meant, in effect, building new versions of the old cars. "The tubs were the same, but the gearboxes were different," Bobby explains, "and it became almost like a black hole that the more you did, the more you had to do, and you could never get out of it."

Bobby qualified thirteenth and finished sixth at the 1993 season opener in Surfers Paradise. He qualified seventh at Phoenix, then struggled in the race and pulled out because the handling was spooky. This, remember, was a race Bobby had dominated twelve months earlier. At Long Beach, he qualified tenth and finished a distant second to Paul Tracy after many of the front-runners hit trouble. The result belied the car's shortcomings, which became painfully evident during the month of May.

While Bobby got down to business in the Lola, Groff was given the task of racing the RH01 in six of the remaining races. Here he pushes the recalcitrant RH01, painted in Miller Light livery, around the Milwaukee Mile. His best finish was a ninth at Portland. (Dan Boyd)

Bobby struggled all month at Indianapolis practice and qualifying, driving over his head on occasion, in an effort to find speed. On the first weekend of qualifying he scraped into the field, twenty-fifth fastest, 6.7 MPH slower than pole winner Arie Luyendyk. It was clear that other drivers would likely eclipse Bobby's speed over the second weekend of qualifying and bump him from the starting field. Consequently, he spent the second week of practice toiling to find competitive qualifying speed from his backup RH01 rather than preparing for the race.

On the second qualifying weekend, with fewer than 15 minutes to go on the last day of qualifying, Bobby was bumped by Eddie Cheever. Aboard his backup RH01, Bobby went out just one minute before the closing gun, the last man to try to make the field that year. He drove his heart out, but after a reasonable first lap, the car's front end skated scarily wide on the second lap, and the lack of grip got worse with each of Bobby's four qualifying laps. He was slower than the week before. He failed to make the race, ending two of the toughest weeks of his life.

"The car wasn't bad," Bobby says, "but we just didn't have the resources, whether it was time, people, or money, and our failure to understand that was really the failure of the project. I have the greatest respect for Don Halliday, but some of the problem was the fact that Don wasn't able to really organize everything and hold to deadlines. There were time limits set that weren't held to, and that's just death when you're developing a car. Some of it was the fact that it took so much time to replenish our stocks with spares for the old car, let alone create something for the new car. And the wind tunnel was screwed up, but it was just one of those things that you didn't really understand until you got into it, but the further you went into it, the messier it got."

Hogan says he learned some lessons from the failure. "I've never second-guessed a decision over time," Hogan shrugs. "It was one of those things where you take a gamble, and we did, and it didn't work out, and we got out of it. But it was tough, and not making Indy, that was really a very, very tough month.

"I think if I had to do it over, I wouldn't have decided to build a car and then race it the same year. I think I would say, OK, if we're going to build a car, let's test it for a year. We would do some back-to-back testing. I think Bobby would agree that's one of the things we should have done."

After failing to qualify at Indianapolis, Bobby and Hogan decided to shelve the RH01 project. The car was driven in six races over the balance of the season by second driver, Mike Groff, who had been otherwise busy that summer. He had been track-testing Honda's new Indy engine that had finally been developed as a result of Bobby's urgings.

Bobby waits with Nigel Mansell and Mario Andretti for practice to start at Phoenix. Mansell, the reigning F1 World Champion, had left the Williams F1 team to join Andretti at Newman-Haas Racing for 1993. At Phoenix, Mansell crashed heavily in practice and missed the race. Despite his rough start, he went on to win the 1993 PPG Cup. (Rahal collection)

Aboard a new Lola, Bobby immediately bounced back at Milwaukee the week after the Indy 500, finishing fourth, and he produced a series of strong results over the rest of the year. His best race was near the season's end in Vancouver, where he finished second to Al Unser Jr. and ultimately salvaged fourth place in the championship behind Nigel Mansell, Emerson Fittipaldi, and Paul Tracy. Groff raced one of the unloved RH01s for the last time at Mid-Ohio in September, then the car was retired, never to be seen again.

"Would we do it again?" Bobby asks. "Even at the time, I thought that there was no real reason why you would build your own car, although certainly there is the concept that building your own car is an advantage. But we were designing the new car to work with the Honda engine. Don Halliday and I met with the Honda people in California, and we were going to design this new chassis around the engine, so there seemed to be some sense to it in that respect.

"I think the only real value, one strong reason to do it again, is if you had an engine program with somebody where that engine—its size, weight, or whatever—could be taken advantage of, whereas buying a chassis off the shelf would not take advantage of it.

"It would always have to be a parallel program for me. You should never do it and rest everything on that, because you cannot build and develop a car in the heat of combat."

Once again, Bobby enjoyed a pretty good weekend in Toronto. He qualified third and finished fourth behind Paul Tracy, Emerson Fittipaldi, and Danny Sullivan. (Michael C. Brown)

197

"The first year we were really miserable."

After experimenting with and discarding the concept of building its own chassis in 1993, Rahal-Hogan would conduct another experiment in 1994. This time the team planned to race a new engine from Honda, which had won a series of world championships over the years, first in Grand Prix motorcycle racing, then in Formula One car racing. Bobby had, of course, been instrumental in pushing Honda to go Indy car racing. In fact, it's not too bold to suggest that had it not been for Bobby's efforts over many years to introduce Honda to Indy car racing, it's unlikely the Japanese motorcycle and car manufacturer ever would have competed in CART.

At the Detroit Auto Show in January of 1993, Honda announced it was going Indy car racing, starting with the 1994 season. The original plan had been to design the engine to suit the Truesports, or RH chassis, and toward that end Don Halliday met several times with Honda Performance and Development general manager Robert Clarke and engineers from

Above: Honda engine designer Toshinari Sonoda had been involved with the Japanese manufacturer's successful Formula One attack from 1984 through 1992. Sonoda and his colleagues discovered that Indy car racing was more difficult than they thought. (Paul Webb)

Opposite: Bobby and his engineers glumly try to figure out what to do next in the pit lane at Indianapolis. For the second year in a row, he failed to qualify for the 500, although this time partner Hogan had a backup plan. On the second weekend, Bobby and Groff qualified a pair of Lola-Ilmors. (Michael C. Brown)

After getting encouraging results from the Honda engine during their 1993 development program, Bobby and Hogan were confident that the 1994 season would be a successful one when they arrived for testing at Sebring in February. (Dan Boyd)

Honda R&D. With the failure of the RH project, however, that part of the equation was erased from the board. Bobby and Groff would race Lola-Hondas in 1994.

Learning to understand the Japanese culture and working with Honda was an interesting experience for Bobby. He recalls an early meeting with the R&D staff at the Wako research facility, one of four Honda R&D centers in Japan, in which he found himself a literal focal point of their inquiries about Indy car racing.

"I'll never forget walking into this big room, and there was a huge U-shaped table," Bobby relates. "And I see fifteen chairs on one side of the U, and there's only one chair on the other side. So everybody sits down, and I'm at the one seat, on my own, and everybody is looking at me, just grinning. It was my job to inform them, to perform, to regale them, I guess, if possible.

"The Japanese have meeting areas," he adds, "and then they have meeting areas. The general meeting area is where they bring people from the outside. It's a very comfortable living room setting—sofas, a table, water, something to eat, maybe. But this particular meeting room at Wako was very sterile."

Bobby had enjoyed an insider's look at Ferrari in Italy five years earlier, and his distinction between Ferrari's and Honda's R&D operations is very clear. "The Japanese are much

Bobby examines technical data sheets with both his team and Honda's engineers. Program manager Michihiro Asaka is to the right with his back to the camera. (Paul Webb)

vest $750 million for a 44 percent stake in USAir. That deal collapsed after the United States and Britain failed to agree on steps to permit greater competition for their airlines. Andrew H. Card, Secretary of Transportation, then said he was prepared to reject the deal.

The proposal also calls for Air Canada and Air Partners to each select six directors for Continental's 18-member board. The transaction is expected to be completed this month.

Mr. Card said that his agency's approval of the Continental deal "re-

security.

Senator John C. Danforth, a Missouri Republican, asked Mr. Pena about the prospect of permitting larger foreign stakes in United States carriers.

Mr. Danforth said that "access to

Associated Press

A prototype Indianapolis 500 race car that would use a new Honda engine was introduced yesterday in Detroit by Thomas G. Elliott, executive vice president of the American Honda Motor Company.

Honda to Build Engines for Indy Race Cars

By DORON P. LEVIN

Special to The New York Times

DETROIT, Jan. 7 — Eager to portray itself more convincingly as an American institution, the Honda Motor Company's United States subsidiary said today that it would begin building engines for race cars in the Indianapolis 500 and associated races, starting in 1994.

Honda executives said they expected the racing program to help in the marketing of Honda and Acura cars and to provide racing experience for the company's American engineers and technicians.

Honda especially wants to improve its sales in the nation's heartland, where the sentiment for buying American products runs high, said Thomas G. Elliott, executive vice president of the American Honda Motor Company.

Honda's announcement came a day after it suffered a sales setback in the United States, as the company's Accord yielded first place in American sales to the Ford Taurus after leading for three years running.

In the beginning, the racing program will consist of supplying engines to a single race team. A month ago, the Nissan Motor Company said it intended to participate in Indy races, but provided few specifics.

Chevrolet Has Been Dominant

For several years, the PPG Indy-car racing series and the Indianapolis 500, the nation's quintessential motor race, have been dominated by engines sponsored by Chevrolet. During a month of trials, nearly a million fans travel to Indianapolis, and the race receives nationwide coverage.

Although Honda operates several plants in Ohio and research and administrative offices in California, it has found that it is often perceived as simply an importer. In fact, the majority of the cars Honda sells in the United States are American made, and it sells more cars in North America than in Japan.

Last month, the Big Three ejected Honda from the Motor Vehicle Manu-

facturers Association, the American industry's trade group, because it was often at odds with the trade group's political goals.

Honda experienced great success building engines for Formula One race cars before deciding last year to pull out because of the high costs. The rules governing Formula One do not rule out some exotic technologies, while Indy rules tend to keep technologies and expenses in check.

"Challenges have always been important to the growth and success of Honda," Mr. Elliott said. Unlike the Chevrolet engines that are built and maintained mostly by non-Chevy personnel, Honda prefers to use its own technicians and engineers.

Typically, an Indy racing team buys engines and chassis from different makers, and Honda has no plan to build a chassis. Rumors have circulated in racing circles that Bobby Rahal, winner of the 1986 Indy 500 and a team owner who also owns a Honda dealership in Mechanicsburg, Pa., will be the first to use the Honda engine, a 6.5-liter, twin-turbo V-8.

ly for
stpone
hange
(Reuters)

JOBS

many as
nion of
ources it
d come
nan de-
eople
The
ance

hs after
ad been
f reor-
n an ef-
ading
(AP)

RES

mil-
e

Chev-
Texas.
rter of
take.
ce
t in-
nds
vron
ster-
(AP)

ED

aker,

er
d ex-
s

25,
ews)

s
m-
t
at
r

oe-
rs)

I.B
Th
A

The
chines
executi
sion-ma
are vie
succeed

The t
Ned C.
Toole.
chief ex
now se
Lautenb
likely su

Mr. T
manufa
55 years
strong c
executiv
accordii
Akers,
reaches
be some
for seve

Analy
politics
addition
and the
speed o
from big
compute
assaults
I.B.M. by

To cop
tables ha
moves m
ing the
manager
an analy
San Fran

Mr. La
dent and
North A
and serv
States an
manager
and mai
AS400 sy
midrange
last 18 m
engineere
IBM Nor

Mr. La
ident, is
N.Y., he
where w
Pacific. P
included
bution di
and over
I.B.M.'s p
in the mid
makers g

more secretive and organized," he observes. "Ferrari was like a junkyard of engines, whereas Honda was very tidy, very orderly. There was genuine passion there, like there was at Ferrari, but at Honda, science ruled."

Honda's first CART engine had only run on the dyno in 1990. It was an aluminum-block engine built by Mugen, a separate, Honda-owned engine-building company, and was used to establish some baseline engineering data. In 1992, work had continued on the first aluminum-block Honda Indy V-8, code-named FEX, and the following year, Bobby had set up a separate "skunk works" shop in Columbus, about 10 miles away from Rahal-Hogan headquarters, in order to maintain a Honda-powered Lola test car and keep it separate from his conventional, Ilmor-equipped operation, lest he upset anyone at Ilmor.

The skunk works operation was run by Dennis Swan, now CART's vice president of logistics, and Bobby's number two, Mike Groff, was given the job of test driver. In addition to racing the unloved, ex-Truesports RH01 for much of that year, Groff pounded 'round and 'round for Honda, putting more than 5,000 test miles on the engine that summer.

"Actually, that first engine was a very good engine," Bobby says. "But there was a big internal battle between Honda R&D and Mugen, and the engine we finally raced was not as good as the engine we had tested. We tested at Indianapolis with Mike in 1993, and I remember—this is hilarious if you really think about it, because we were so pleased—it was June or July, and it was hot. I said, 'I don't want anybody to know how fast this thing really is.' So we put download into the car, and Mike was running 221, 222 MPH with so much drag it's not funny. A year later we went back and were not even close to that speed. We were just struggling to find speed, and 219 was about as fast as it would go."

In February of 1993, Robert Clarke joined Honda to run the company's Performance & Development engine shop in Santa Clarita, California. "There was a chief engineer running the project at Mugen who had one way of thinking, and another chief engineer at R&D who

hadn't been involved in the early development of the Mugen who had his own ideas," Clarke explains. "The FEX originally was an aluminum-block engine, but it failed miserably in dyno tests, developing cracks all through the block, and they didn't really know what to do. The first thing they did was try to strengthen the block by adding more ribs and more material, but it just moved the cracks to a different place."

As a result, Honda reverted to a cast-iron block, like their successful F1 engines of the time. "It was a major decision," Clarke says of the difference of opinion between

Honda R&D and Mugen. "The thinking was that there is very little weight penalty in using cast iron because the wall thicknesses and ribbing are so much less than in an aluminum-block engine. The other thing was that Honda had a lack of understanding of V-8 engine design in general, and a total lack of understanding of oval racing and the stresses that are put on the engine on an oval. What was happening was the whole block was twisting, which was destroying the bearings and crankshaft and connecting rods. In the end, a huge billet-steel girdle was put on the bottom of the engine to hold it all together."

At the end of 1993, after a summer of encouraging track testing, Bobby went to Japan to discuss details of Honda's debut season in CART with Asaka and Honda's president, Nobuhiko Kawamoto. "Debi and I had dinner with Mr. Asaka and Mr. Kawamoto at a very nice restaurant, and we were having a very good time, and it was nice to see Mr. Kawamoto. He's very effusive, very outgoing, and speaks English very well. Of course, he was one of the first guys on the original Honda F1 program in 1963, and he lived in England, and he's a very worldly man.

Bobby gets ready to test the revised engine. Honda had produced a series of detail changes in an effort to get its program on the right track. After all the problems with the RH01 the previous year, it was extremely difficult to go through a trying season with Honda. (Paul Webb)

"We ordered a nice bottle of red wine and we toasted, and Mr. Asaka said, 'To win every race next year.' And Mr. Kawamoto said, 'No, no. To *finish* every race next year.' I guess I bought into Mr. Asaka's view. Maybe I should have been more of a realist there."

It turned out that the wise Kawamoto had the correct perspective on 1994. It was a year of deep frustration for Bobby, his team, and Honda.

"The thing that colored the Honda project in a lot of respects for us was the Truesports project because we went to Indy in 1993 and didn't qualify," Bobby says. "Then a year later, Scott Roembke and Tim Cindric came to me about three or four weeks before opening day at the 500 and they said, 'We need to think about what we're going to do when we don't qualify.' And I said, 'What do you mean, when we don't qualify? I think we'll qualify, no problem. But they said to look at the number of cars out there, and it was iffy based on our testing times and the fact that there were a lot of one-offs [teams that raced only at Indianapolis], like Dick Simon's running five cars, all Ford-powered. And I thought, 'Oh no, here we go again.'

"Had we qualified for the 500 in 1993, that might have made all the difference in the world," Bobby adds, "but having not qualified in 1993, we could not just sit there. I don't think Carl or I felt comfortable at all going to Miller and saying, 'Sorry guys, but our Honda program is not working like we thought, and we're going to miss this race, too.' I mean, how much can you expect of your sponsor?"

Fortunately, Hogan had anticipated the situation and had already orchestrated a switch to Penske-Ilmors for Bobby and teammate Groff to use for the second weekend of qualifying at Indianapolis and the race. "Honda was very demanding and thought the problem was not the engine; it was us or the car," Hogan says. "It was a tough decision to make, but that's what we had to do. We had not made the race the year before. Miller was very good about it in 1993. They supported us. Jack MacDonough, who's now the president of Miller, said he always thought there were two ways to get a lot of headlines. One was to win the race, and the second was to crash. 'You guys have developed a third,' he said, 'and that is not to make the race!'

Opposite: The Honda engine debuted at Surfers Paradise. Bobby was hit on the start and broke his front wing. The guylines the team rigged to support the wing (visible between the nose and end plates) kept it attached to the car. At the next turn, the wing got caught under the front wheel and sent Bobby into a tire wall. (Michael C. Brown)

Left: Mike Groff joins Hogan and Bobby for a preseason team photo. Groff's car was sponsored by Motorola in 1994, and with the new Honda engines, everyone was full of optimism for the coming season. (George Tiedemann/ Rahal collection)

Bobby had an encouraging race at Detroit's street circuit, where he both qualified and finished sixth. Nevertheless, the relationship between Honda and Rahal-Hogan was becoming increasingly strained, and though there was no discernible increase in power, the engine's reliability was unaccountably deteriorating. (Dan Boyd)

"That was a good attitude," Hogan goes on, "and they had supported us so much that in 1994, I just felt if we didn't make the race, I wouldn't have blamed any of our sponsors if they just absolutely pulled the plug on us. So that's when we made the big switch to Penske-Ilmors for the race.

"At one point we realized we weren't going to qualify, and I asked Bobby what was our alternative," Hogan says. "There was about a 15-second pause, and he looked at me and said, 'You.' And I said, 'What do you mean?' He said, 'Well, you always come up with things. I'm counting on you.' I sort of got a kick out of that, because he didn't know I was already working on it.

"I think part of my role was to bring the balance of what responsibilities we had to the sponsors, to the driver, to the crew. I had made the deal on the cars with Roger because we knew each other so well, and I think Bobby was shocked that I was able to do that. I had talked to Roger and set it up as a possibility before Bobby knew it, because he was driving and I was taking care of the business and technical stuff. But when I came to him and told him, he was very pleased that we had an alternative."

HPD general manager Clarke tells the story from Honda's perspective. "I remember it well," Clarke says with a half-grin. "I arrived on the Thursday before the first weekend of qualifying and walked over to the Honda trailer, and everyone was in an uproar because Mike Groff had just crashed. The bottom end had let go, and he spun on his own oil and crashed. Carl Hogan was quite agitated, and Bobby and he called me over to their motor home, and that was the first time we began to understand that Carl was planning a backup plan. We were a little upset with that idea, and we reached an agreement that they would not pull the cars out of the qualifying line, that they would wait until they were bumped from the field before they went to another car. But after Mike qualified, they pulled Bobby's car."

Under traditional Indianapolis qualifying rules, a driver was permitted three atttempts at the four-lap qualifying run in different cars. After Groff qualified, but at a speed that was almost sure to be bumped out of the fastest thirty-three by subsequent qualifiers, Bobby decided to pull his car out of the qualifying line rather than risk wasting one of his three attempts.

It was a tense time. Looking back on it, Bobby says, "If I was really to get nasty about it, I'd say if anybody let anybody down, Honda let Bobby Rahal and Rahal-Hogan down because they just weren't ready."

Honda president Nobuhiko Kawamoto and American Honda executive vice-president Tom Elliott were on hand at the season-opening race at Surfers Paradise to witness the Honda engine's debut. (Michael C. Brown)

After finishing an encouraging third in the race at Indianapolis aboard one of the two rented Penske-Ilmors, Bobby reverted to racing Lola-Hondas for the rest of the year, struggling at most races to qualify in the top twenty. He kept pushing for Honda to build an aluminum engine.

"They told me they would not build an aluminum engine," Bobby insists, even though a parallel development program of the new aluminum HRH engine had begun in secret. "'That's not our way,' they always said. Even the Formula One engine, when they were V-10s, were all cast-iron blocks. Only when they went to a V-12 did they go to magnesium blocks, because a V-12 was so heavy in cast iron, and even then they were throwing blocks away after every race.

"We tried to convince them that the engine was heavy. I think a normal Ilmor at the time, fitted out with the clutch, was 260 pounds or thereabouts, and the Honda was 340! In fact, they came up with a flat-crank engine in the middle of 1994, and it weighed even more than the other one because they had to stiffen the whole bottom end. It kept throwing rods and running through rod bearings. That's why the engines kept blowing up at Indy that year, and Mike had a crash as a result of one of those blowups. There were a lot of problems."

Right: With a new flat-crank engine, Bobby finished second at Toronto behind Michael Andretti. "We ended up where we did not because the power was better, but because the car handled extremely well," Bobby says. "And really, the *lack* of power was an advantage to some degree, in putting the power down smoothly."

Opposite: Although Honda went on to dominate CART in 1996, 1997, and 1998, Bobby refuses to second-guess the decision he made in 1995 to split with the Japanese manufacturer. "I knew the path that we were taking was not going to make it," Bobby says. (Paul Webb)

Hogan adds to Bobby's assessment. "They had an iron block and it was about 80 pounds overweight," Hogan says. "The weight was at the top end, which threw out the whole balance of the car. The car wasn't designed for that. Also, for some reason, the engine was overheating a little bit. So we had to take the shutters off the radiator exits, and without the shutters we lost aerodynamics.

"I had a serious discussion with one of the lead Honda people. I said, 'When will you build an aluminum engine?' And his comment to me was, 'We will never build an aluminum engine.' I said, 'Why?' and they said iron is stronger than aluminum. And it was right then and there that I felt we would never be competitive."

HPD manager Clarke disagrees with the views presented by Bobby and Hogan. "The development of the HRH engine, the generation after the FEX, really started after the failure to qualify at Indy," Clarke says. "The next week, things started to roll in organizing a new team, with more people involved with the project and a new chief engineer. From that point on it became a parallel program of ongoing development for the FEX and new development for the HRH." American Honda vice president Elliott adds to Clarke's comments. "The aluminum engine was under development, but it couldn't be ready until 1996, and they probably wanted it for 1995," Elliott says.

Honda's former president, Kawamoto, started his engineering career with the company as a racing mechanic in Europe in the '60s with Honda's first Formula Two engines and F1 cars. Kawamoto ran Honda for six years before retiring in the spring of 1998, and he admits that Bobby was essentially right about what Honda needed to do to become competitive.

"The first year we were really miserable," Kawamoto concedes. "We certainly noticed that Indy car racing was really professional. Maybe sometimes it's much more professional and more difficult to win than Formula One, because the regulations are so strict. So we changed our attitude. We said, 'OK, let's try it as a professional activity for the second year.' And we put all our effort into designing and producing a very serious engine for 1995."

In the middle of 1994, Bobby made the toughest decision of his professional life: He turned his back on Honda in order to offer a stronger hope to his partners and sponsors of being capable of running at the sharp end of the field in 1995. After so much time and effort, Bobby's decision to end his partnership with Honda was a bitter pill to swallow.

Laguna Seca, the final
race of 1994, was
Bobby's last drive with
Honda. His race came to
a disappointingly quick
end amid a first-lap
collision with Michael
Andretti. (Jon Eisberg)

He had spent more than five years massaging and cajoling both Honda and American Honda into pursuing an Indy car engine-building program, but he and partner Hogan decided to reject Honda engines for the 1995 season and switch to Mercedes-Benz. After Mid-Ohio in August, Bobby sadly informed Asaka that his team wouldn't continue with Honda.

"I had worked on this project for so long, and I had developed a very close personal relationship with Mr. Asaka, as well as other people at Honda. And I had Carl and Miller talking to me, although I have to say, in Miller's defense, they never once said to us, 'Get rid of them, or we're out.' But they didn't have to. I understood and Carl understood full well what Miller's approach was. They didn't give a damn what engine or what car you had. All they cared about was that you were in the race and you were running for the lead.

"The upshot was that Carl and I finally decided enough was enough," Bobby says. "Financially, it was a huge deal to us. It might have been a big deal with Honda, but it could have been our *last* deal with Miller. It was a very hard decision to make."

Bobby felt the team had developed its car into a good-handling but underpowered racer. They had managed a second-place finish at Toronto, then at Mid-Ohio Bobby qualified seventh and was running about sixth, then the engine broke. "I got out of the car, and I was steaming and probably said some things I shouldn't have said about how frustrating it was," recalls Bobby.

After the Mid-Ohio race, Asaka visited Bobby in his office at the shop. "I had to be straight with him," Bobby says. "I told him the situation was very bad. And he said, 'What if we sponsor you?' Well, of course, I had a five-year deal with Miller and I had other sponsors and commitments, and I wasn't about to just say, 'See ya.' Honda was just part of the puzzle. I didn't want to be beholden to a single entity. That was one of the reasons I started my own team. And I said to Mr. Asaka, 'I can't do that.' And that was the end of a beautiful relationship.

"I said, 'I'm sorry.' I don't know why I was apologizing, other than I felt like I was breaking a trust, a friendship, because obviously this was going to have a major effect on my relationship with Mr. Asaka and anybody at Honda. We had one of the most successful dealerships in the Honda family, and the racing program was elevating me to a level that other dealers didn't have, and yet here I had just forsaken and embarrassed them, even though it might have been their problem."

Bobby is proud of the role he played in Honda's move into Champ car racing, and refuses to second-guess his decision to split with Honda. "I don't look back and say, 'Well, geez, what if?' In some respects, it was one of those important learning experiences in life that you go through, and you need to chalk it up to experience. I think what struck me the most, the deepest sense of failure and disappointment, was how much

Later in the summer, Bobby had to tell his friend Michihiro Asaka the bad news that Rahal-Hogan would not continue with Honda in 1995. After investing so many years in the project, this was perhaps the toughest decision of Bobby's racing life. (Paul Webb)

time and effort and money I had invested in that deal, and then in 1995 other people were enjoying the fruit of it."

It is ironic that through all this turmoil, Honda was undergoing serious scrutiny by CART and the media for attempting to dominate the sport with money. Honda spends a larger portion of its profits on research and development than any other automobile manufacturer. It proved the power of its commitment by winning six straight F1 World Constructors Championships between 1986 and 1991. As a result of its record, many in CART thought Honda would simply outspend and outengineer the opposition. These fears were voiced openly by CART teams that believed they had no chance of ever enjoying Honda engines.

During this period, CART developed its engine supply rules, which require that, once proven a competitive entity, engine manufacturers must supply at least three teams and six cars with engines. Since then this rule has become one of CART's great strengths and has resulted in a full field of closely matched cars powered by Ford-Cosworth, Honda, Mercedes-Benz, and Toyota engines.

Even so, Honda went on to become the dominant CART powerplant in the late 1990s. Starting with Andre Ribeiro's first Honda victory at New Hampshire in August of 1995, Honda-powered drivers would win thirty-one CART races through the end of 1998. Powered by aluminum-block HRH and HRG Honda engines, Jimmy Vasser and Alex Zanardi swept CART's 1996, 1997, and 1998 PPG Cup titles for Chip Ganassi's team, a great achievement for Honda and the team.

"The FEX in 1995 was still cast-iron, but it was an extremely competitive engine," comments American Honda's Elliott. "Andre won at New Hampshire, and Scott Goodyear led at Indy that year until the mess-up near the end with the pace car [when Goodyear anticipated the green flag on a restart and passed the pace car under the yellow]. Adds HPD's Clarke: "It's not true that we didn't appreciate or understand the effect of the added weight. We had to make a decision between holding the engine together and finishing a race and adding weight. Obviously, we knew the compromises being made, but it was more important to have an engine that held together and finished races."

The team prepares to fly to Indianapolis in Bobby's King Air. From left to right: American Honda's Robert Clarke, Bobby, Toshinari Sonoda, Michihiro Asaka, Don Halliday, and Hiroshi Abe. (Rahal collection)

"How many people have said to me, 'Do you regret giving up the Honda deal?' Bobby says in reflection. "Well, at the time, I was glad I did, in a reticent sort of way, because I knew the path we were taking was not going to make it. It was a huge disappointment, but I think we learned some things from it. I think our relationship with Ford is a reflection of that experience to some degree. It's one of those things that if you look back, maybe it was an opportunity squandered, but you've got to do what's best at the time. You can't second-guess those decisions."

Bobby lines up with the rest of the drivers for a group picture at the 1994 season-ending race at Laguna Seca. (Paul Webb)

"It was a very personal situation."

After all the trouble, effort, and heartache expended with the RH01 in 1993 and Honda in 1994, the 1995 season looked like a fresh start for Rahal-Hogan Racing. In many ways, it was a case of going back to basics as the team faced 1995 with the same essential equipment as in its championship-winning 1992 season—Lola chassis, Ilmor engines, now badged as Mercedes-Benz, and Goodyear tires. Bobby talked to Ford about racing the new Cosworth XB engine, which debuted with Newman-Haas and Chip Ganassi's team in 1992, but returned in the end to Ilmor and its new partner, Mercedes-Benz. The reasoning behind his choice of engines for 1995 and 1996 wasn't as obvious as it might seem.

At Indianapolis in 1994, the Penske team had utterly dominated, as Al Unser Jr. won handily after teammate Emerson Fittipaldi crashed in the closing laps. Both were powered by single-camshaft 209-cubic-inch Mercedes-Benz engines. The single-cam engine had been developed in great secrecy by Ilmor Engineering, as Mario Ilien took advantage of USAC's equivalency formula to design an engine specifically for Penske's use at Indianapolis in 1994. CART had expunged any engine equivalencies from its rule book many years earlier. The USAC rules for the Indy 500, however, permitted single-camshaft engines with pushrod-operated valves to have 50 cubic inches more than the more conven-

Above: Brazilian veteran Raul Boesel replaced Groff as Bobby's teammate at Rahal-Hogan for the 1995 season driving a car sponsored by Duracell, but he did not enjoy a very successful year. (Loren Hosack/Rahal collection)

Opposite: At Long Beach, Bobby qualified sixth, but his transmission failed two-thirds of the way through the race. Al Unser Jr. won the event for the fifth time, with Scott Pruett second and Teo Fabi third. (Paul Webb)

After rejecting Honda, Bobby did some serious thinking about who the best engine supplier would be for his team in the future. He talked at length with Ford, but decided for a variety of reasons (including USAC's Indy engine rules) to go with Mercedes-Benz for 1995. (Paul Webb)

tional turbocharged 160-cubic-inch four-camshaft engines built by Ford-Cosworth, Honda, and Ilmor.

"We had all seen what had happened at the Speedway in 1994," Bobby says, "and the biggest question for us became what would happen with the rules for Indy and the availability of the pushrod 209 engine. I had a relationship with Ford in the early '80s in running the IMSA program, and I had gotten to know Dan Rivard [who, by 1994, was Ford's racing boss], and I had a lot of respect for him.

"Just prior to the Detroit race in '94, we went to see him about what was going on with Ford. Both Carl and I were leaning toward the Ford program. We knew that the XB was a better and more powerful engine than the Ilmor D engine, but certainly with time the D was going to get better. But we gave the pushrod aspect of it a lot of weight in our decision, and we asked Ford if they planned to build a single-camshaft engine, and they said they didn't have any plans to do so.

"Regrettably, I had to say to Dan that we had to make a different choice. I think the Ford people were concerned that we weren't actually serious. I think they questioned what the fallout would have been had they told us they had a pushrod engine on the drawing board, which they actually did. Cosworth had gone a fair way with the design, and they didn't want their secret out of the bag."

In the end, the Rahal-Hogan team chose Ilmor as their engine supplier because they were told they would be able to get the pushrod engine. Assuming that the rules would stay the same at Indianapolis, they had to have a pushrod engine because the Ford XB and regular Ilmor would not be competitive.

But the rules at Indianapolis did change. USAC twice changed the boost rules in order to render the pushrod engine noncompetitive in 1995. The rule changes took place over a period of many months, which delayed the engine manufacturers and teams in making decisions about what to race at Indy in 1995. When Ilmor and Mercedes finally canceled the pushrod engine because the Speedway had changed the rules, Rahal-Hogan had already made their commitments. Of course, this kind of vacillation on the part of USAC and the Indianapolis Motor Speedway played a large part in the growing rift between CART and the Speedway's president, Tony George.

With the reliable Lola-Mercedes/Goodyear combination, Bobby was again extremely competitive. He was third in the 1995 season-opener, a street circuit in downtown Miami run only that year by CART, and second at Surfers Paradise. He finished third at Indianapolis after being in the hunt all the way, was third again at Portland in June, and was second in downtown Toronto in July. There were no wins, however, and too many DNFs (did not finish) to contend seriously for the championship, although at forty-two years old, Bobby was as competitive as ever, and he finished third in the championship behind twenty-four-year-old Formula One–bound Jacques Villeneuve and thirty-three-year-old Al Unser Jr.

Brazilian veteran Raul Boesel replaced Mike Groff as Bobby's teammate in 1995. Boesel ran well in some races and had his best day of the year in Portland, where he finished fifth. Bobby and the team liked Raul and believed a second year together would have yielded stronger results, but Boesel decided to go with Brazilian beer giant Brahma, which had big plans for 1996 with 1995 CART champion Team Green.

Meanwhile, at the beginning of 1995, Bobby had made another big decision of his own. After wrestling with the decision for some time, he finally determined to split with partner Carl Hogan and go it alone as a team owner. He would bring in late-night talk show host and friend David Letterman as a minority partner and operate as his own man. Hogan learned of Bobby's intentions in the middle of 1995 and was not pleased by Bobby's decision, which would take effect at the end of the year. Since then, the former partners have been little more than civil with each other.

By the middle of 1995, Carl Hogan had learned that at the end of the season Bobby would become an independent team owner, with David Letterman as a minority partner. Hogan was upset by Bobby's decision, and the second half of the season was tense as communication between the two all but ended. (Art Flores)

Above: The latest Ilmor-designed Mercedes-Benz turbo V-8 is installed in the back of one of Bobby's 1995 Lolas. He had expected to race the 209-cubic-inch single-cam Mercedes engine at Indianapolis in 1995, but a series of USAC rule changes killed that possibility. (Dan Boyd)

Right: Bobby at speed on the Portland International Raceway road course. He finished third at this race behind 1994 champion Al Unser Jr. and 1995 champion-to-be Jimmy Vasser. (Paul Webb)

"I'm afraid to say it was definitely an acrimonious split," Bobby admits. "Carl's feelings were hurt, there's no question. I would say it became a very personal situation, not so much from my point of view but from his. And it's a shame because had it not been for Carl, Rahal-Hogan might never have started. By the same token, Carl made out quite well in our relationship.

"The move was made strictly because over time I felt that I wanted to have more control over what was going to happen in the future. I think that with Carl, hard feelings probably still exist, and I guess I, too, could have cause for hard feelings, but I'm the kind of person that says, 'What's done is done. Let's go forward and make the best of it.' My interest is not to drag dirt back up or to make myself somehow sound more virtuous at the expense of others.

"I guess the overriding thing is and was, I want to have the controlling voice. I think Carl's and my ultimate objectives were a little different. That's not blaming anybody. That's just illuminating the reality, I think. But having said that, I think it's enough cause to try to do your own thing.

"I've personally struggled because of that decision to take it over, because it cost a lot of money. And it had an effect on certain aspects of our business. But I look at it as just making

an investment. In business, someone has to put up money or do something to get something going, and in effect, I was doing nothing more than that.

"I'm sad for Carl. Carl is a good guy, and it's a shame the lack of luck and results that he's had as of late. But Carl's a racer. When we won at Nazareth in 1992, it was because he rolled the dice and called some great strategy. I think he needs to find somebody who's willing to be Carl's partner as a driver. If Carl can find somebody like me as I was in 1991, I think he can still see a lot of success."

Hogan's displeasure with Bobby remains undiminished. "My view hasn't changed at all," Hogan says grimly. "I was very disappointed in Bobby. He had wanted to bring David Letterman in as some kind of a part-owner. I told him in the off-season that I didn't think it was necessary. I said we had good sponsorship, and he felt we needed a celebrity on the team, and I really wasn't in racing to have celebrities. I guess Bobby was more caught up with that relationship than I was. We talked to David, and he couldn't have been nicer. I really like him. There was no problem there.

"I think Bobby felt like he was a driver, and he had to look at what was best for him. But I put a lot of money into the operation, and I felt that Bobby couldn't have started the team without me."

As in many divorces, it was impossible for both parties to see things from the same perspective, and Hogan feels he was blindsided by Bobby. "I don't know how it would have worked out if Bobby had come and said, 'We want to dissolve this at the end of the year, Carl,'" he ruminates. "I was hurt by the way he did it. Very truthfully, I think there are a lot

of other owners who understand that, because if they were in the same position, they wouldn't have liked this.

"You know, Bobby and I live with each other," Hogan says. "The past is the past. I think we've been very civil to each other. I wouldn't do a thing to try to hurt him, and I really feel that he wouldn't do anything to hurt me. I think we're both making the best of the situation and going forward."

Despite his criticism of Bobby, Hogan remains very complimentary about Rahal the racing driver. "I think Bobby was a very unique race driver," Hogan comments, "because he was very methodical and very programmed, and sometimes when you thought the car could be running just a little bit faster, you realized that what he was doing was driving very smart. Sometimes you've got to sit back, and Bobby knew his limit and the car's limit.

"I can tell you why Bobby was always good at Toronto and Vancouver," Hogan goes on. "It's because Bobby was such a precise driver that the walls didn't bother him. The reason I think he didn't do better at Mid-Ohio, for example, is because everybody else was hanging wheels off the road and doing everything to do a fast time, and Bobby stayed on the road just as if there was a wall there. After a while, you began to appreciate his experience, and precision, and clean driving.

"I don't think there was ever a situation that Bobby really didn't try, or where he was scared. I don't think that ever came up in his mind. I think he had a job to do and he did it. I think the only thing that ever happened is that once in a while, Bobby's businesses might have caused some temporary distractions. But he was also smart enough to realize when that happened, and to get back on track."

Hogan went on to form a partnership with old friend and fellow truck leaser Roger Penske for 1996 with Emerson Fittipaldi driving, until Emerson crashed massively in the U.S. 500, breaking his neck and effectively ending his driving career. Hogan then started his own team, running a Reynard-Mercedes for rookie Dario Franchitti in 1997 and signing Finnish ace J.J. Lehto for 1998 and 1999.

During 1995, Bobby had some serious conversations with his friend Adrian Newey about the brilliant designer joining Team Rahal for 1996. At the time, Newey was disillusioned about life with the Williams F1 team and was looking for a change. In the end, Newey decided to join McLaren instead of Team Rahal, and with Mika Hakkinen driving, Newey's McLaren-Mercedes won the 1998 F1 World Championship.

"We always kept in touch, because I developed a real friendship with Adrian. And when I made the decision that I wanted to go off and start Team Rahal, I wanted him to be my partner and to give him an opportunity to have equity, an ownership in the team. If we were ever going to build another car again, I couldn't think of a better guy to actually do it. We

Bobby crests the hill approaching the Corkscrew at Laguna Seca on his way to seventh place in the last race of 1995. Michael Andretti's fourth place was not enough to beat Bobby to third in the championship. (Paul Webb)

talked, and I think he did think seriously of it. He did ask if I was going to go Formula One racing, and I think if I had said yes, he might have gone with us.

"I have nothing but the highest respect for Adrian," Bobby remarks. "I think forgetting the fact that he's a genius, Adrian is a hell of a race car engineer. When I worked with him in 1984 and 1985, he gave me such confidence as a driver that I felt I could move mountains.

Bobby had hoped to persuade old friend Adrian Newey to join his team as a partner and technical director. Newey eventually decided to join the McLaren F1 team, with which his car won the 1998 World Championship with Mika Hakkinen at the wheel. (Steven Tee/LAT Photographic)

"I haven't washed my hands of Adrian," Bobby says. "I think someday he may still want to do Champ cars, but the timing for Adrian with McLaren was such that I told him it was a great offer and he should take it, and that one day, maybe we will get together again. You never know, maybe somebody will come along and say, 'We want an American Formula One team,' and the first guy I'd call would be Adrian."

Newey explains his serious interest in Bobby's 1995 offer and in Champ cars in general. "I stayed close friends with Bobby since we worked together in the early '80s," Newey comments. "Bobby had been very good to me, not only in the engineering sense in terms of his initial patience, but also on the social side. If I went to the States, he would make sure a car was available for me in Columbus. Whatever it might be, he had always been very friendly and helpful.

"I have tremendous respect for Bobby. I get on socially very well with him. I think he has very good values and is an interesting guy to go and have dinner with and have a chat with. You can always have a lively discussion and enjoyable evening, talking about many things, not just motor racing."

Newey had also become very friendly with Bobby's parents, Mike and Barbara, and would occasionally stay with them in Chicago, and Mike would visit Newey whenever he traveled to England.

"At the same time, I'd been through a rather unhappy divorce in 1989, and Bobby and Debi had been quite understanding and supportive through that. Once Bobby had set up his own team, he always said, 'Well, I'd love you to come and work with me, and not only be an engineer but also a partner with a shareholding in the team, if you'd like it.' And I considered it very seriously."

Newey believes the essential difference between CART and F1 is money. "People in Europe say Formula One is more competitive. I think that is a false statement. To me, competition is about doing the best you can with the resources you have available to you, and I think the competitive instinct in Champ car racing is just as just as strong as it is in

Formula One. The difference is the resources are smaller, and from a technical and innovation standpoint that does mean Champ cars are behind Formula One. The budget for research is smaller; therefore, the amount of things you can do is less.

"The cachet of Formula One against Champ cars is not something I'm terribly worried about, but having the extra resources and freedom is something that I actually like about Formula One. That's not saying that in the future I wouldn't like to have another go at Champ car racing, but at the moment I've decided to stay in Formula One."

And in August of 1995, Bobby and Debi moved into a sprawling Georgian mansion in rural New Albany, only a few miles from the Columbus airport and about a 20-minute drive crosstown to the Team Rahal shop. In spring and summer the house is shaded by clusters of tall oak and dogwood trees that surround the property, and in addition to their four children, Michaela, Jarrad, Graham, and Samantha, they have four dogs, four cats, four parrots, and four horses. "Bobby is not the animal lover that I am, but he's very patient about it," Debi says. "He realizes it's a sharing experience for the children. It's a very busy household, but that's the way it should be."

Three of Bobby and Debi's four children join Bobby at the track during a 1995 race weekend. Jarrad (age eight) is in the car with Graham (six) and Samantha (nearly three) on Bobby's lap. Eldest daughter Michaela is absent from the photo. (Dan Boyd)

"I'm in it till they throw me out."

When Team Rahal debuted in 1996, it had changed significantly from its Rahal-Hogan days. First, Bobby's old friend, David Letterman, was on board as a quiet minority partner. Also, Bobby changed chassis manufacturers from Lola to Reynard in his unending search for the optimal technical combination. Reynard had been a very successful small formula car manufacturer for many years, then moved into Champ cars in 1994, and the marque won the very first CART race it entered in Surfers Paradise with Michael Andretti driving for Chip Ganassi's team. In 1995, Reynard had won the CART title, with Barry Green's team and Jacques Villeneuve driving. One last change was that Bryan Herta had been hired to replace the departed Boesel.

Letterman's partnership with Bobby came about through a steadily growing friendship that had developed over a ten-year period. "It was something that we talked about on a number of occasions, but there was never any real impetus to it," Bobby says about the partnership. "David had been approached by a number of people, including Derrick Walker and Vince Granatelli. I said to him at the time, 'David, if you want to come to the races, I'll get you a ticket. Don't feel that the only way you could come to these races is to buy into a team.'

Above: Team Rahal debuted in the 1996 season, with David Letterman as a minority partner. A long-time racing enthusiast, Letterman enjoys his time at the track. Here he celebrates Bobby's second-place finish at Road America. (Dan Boyd)

Opposite: Bobby pulls on his Nomex gloves as he prepares to head onto the track during winter testing at Sebring. To celebrate its twenty-fifth anniversary in racing in 1996, primary sponsor Miller produced a series of different color schemes. (Paul Webb)

CHAPTER

18

Bobby would meet with Letterman whenever there were CART races at the Meadowlands, and Bobby had been on *Late Night* a couple of times. Their friendship developed into a business relationship as well, and as early as 1992, Bobby had invited Letterman to become involved with the RH project.

"There was certainly an uneasiness on Carl's part with the concept of celebrity," Bobby says. "He had been through that years ago with Dick Smothers in Formula 5000, and I always felt that Carl was a little uncomfortable with the attention that I got versus what he got, and he obviously recognized that if David came into the mix, he would get even further down the line."

Though they never entered into a business relationship during the Rahal-Hogan years, Letterman told Bobby that if Bobby were ever to start a team, he would be interested in joining him. "So when I decided to go forward in the middle of '95, I gave David a call and said, 'Are you ready?' And he said, 'Absolutely.' And that was that."

Letterman affirms his long-term commitment to the team. "I'm in it till they throw me out, or until I drop dead in the pits," he remarks. "What I had envisioned for myself was a lovely way to spend spring and summer, but unfortunately, because I'm working forty-eight weeks of the year, I can only come to a few events. My hope is eventually, when the schedule changes, that I can actually show up and enjoy more of the races."

Bryan Herta was twenty-five when he joined the team in 1996. He had won the Indy Lights championship in 1993 with Steve Horne's Tasman team, then in 1994 drove for A.J. Foyt in a season cut short by injury. He returned in 1995 with Chip Ganassi's team. (Dan Boyd)

Letterman is a great fan of racing going back to his childhood days growing up in Indianapolis, and he avidly reads the racing press so that he's intimately familiar with the latest racing news and gossip. "We talk a little bit about the business side of the equation," Bobby says, "but I think David's real interest is the sporting side, although he has expressed on a number of occasions that he'd like to be involved more in the team when his life changes to the point that he has the time to spend. I think David is a little frustrated that the demands of his job really prohibit him from being as involved as he would like. I think that's a frustration for him, and for us, frankly, because we can only grab little snatches of him."

Bobby appreciates the tremendous racing knowledge Letterman brings. "He's very in tune with what's going on, and from a partnership standpoint, I'm sure that's the way it is with Carl Haas and Paul Newman. Paul is very knowledgeable and sophisticated about the sport, and that makes these kinds of partnerships a hell of a lot easier and usually longer lasting."

Bobby's decision to switch from the Lola to the Reynard chassis was a logical one. Reynard Racing Cars has built chassis for every major single-seat formula and, until 1999 when it entered F1, the company had an unmatched record of winning the first race of each new series it competed in. Michael Andretti had kept that streak alive in 1994 when he won the season-opening CART race in Australia, in the Reynard's debut event. Adrian Reynard, the company's

founder, raced Formula Fords in the late 1970s and is now recognized as one of the brightest, most successful car constructors. The British company has twice won the Queen's Award for Export Achievement.

"I've known Bobby a long time, going back to when he raced F3 and F2 in Europe," Reynard says, "and he's a unique sort of guy. He wasn't one of our early converts in that we had to demonstrate to him that we could do it. The fact that he was very loyal to Lola at a time when our car was winning consistently demonstrates a very rare quality, which is loyalty. A lot of team owners would flip as soon as something better comes on the market.

"When he comes over to see our factory, he doesn't just come and make decisions by himself; he involves his team members. They know that at the end of the day he probably will call the shots, but he very much wants to listen to their opinions, he's very careful about the judgments he makes, and he asks all the difficult questions. He's straight in there, to the point. He's highly perceptive, and that's been one of the reasons for his success.

With his car featuring another twenty-fifth anniversary Miller paint scheme, Bobby leads Jimmy Vasser, Al Unser Jr., and Greg Moore at Elkhart Lake. Bobby finished second behind Michael Andretti, and Alex Zanardi was third. (Michael C. Brown)

Left: Adrian Reynard designed, constructed, and drove his first racing car in 1973. His company went on to become one of the largest and most successful chassis manufacturers. Reynard cars won the CART championship in 1995, 1996, 1997, and 1998. (Art Flores)

Zanardi made a spectacular and controversial pass of Herta on
the last lap at the Corkscrew. Zanardi ran wide, off the track,
to complete the maneuver. Some fans loved Zanardi's move;
others thought it was illegal and indefensible. (Rich Chenet)

"Anyone who can actually run a team, own a team, cope with the politics, all the management and sponsor stuff, and drive the car, I have to take my hat off to," Reynard continues. "*I* gave that up in 1979 as being too much. The people I know who can do lots of things simultaneously have very high intellects and are very highly driven. Bobby is a very exceptional person."

Bryan Herta was twenty-five when he replaced Raul Boesel on Team Rahal. He had won the Indy Lights title with Steve Horne's Tasman team in 1993 and drove only five races for A. J. Foyt in his 1994 CART rookie season before crashing heavily and badly breaking his pelvis and right leg in Toronto that summer. Sidelined for the rest of that year, Bryan still walks with a slight limp as a permanent result of his injuries from 1994.

Herta came back in 1995 with Chip Ganassi's team, paired with Jimmy Vasser, and ran the full season for the first time. He had taken his first Champ car pole at Phoenix early in the year and finished a close second to Jacques Villeneuve at Cleveland, beating Jimmy Vasser and Bobby. Villeneuve had passed Herta at the start of the last lap, then went on to steal victory from Michael Andretti after the pair banged wheels in the first turn. Following that race, Ganassi lost all belief in Bryan as a racer. Before the end of the year, Ganassi had determined not to renew Herta, and Bobby quickly decided to sign Bryan to a long-term contract.

"Steve Horne always talked highly of Bryan, and I recommended him to Foyt when he asked me about him," Bobby recalls. "Steve always used to say Bryan reminded him of me. I'm not sure if that's a credit to Bryan or not, but I felt Bryan was a young charger. He

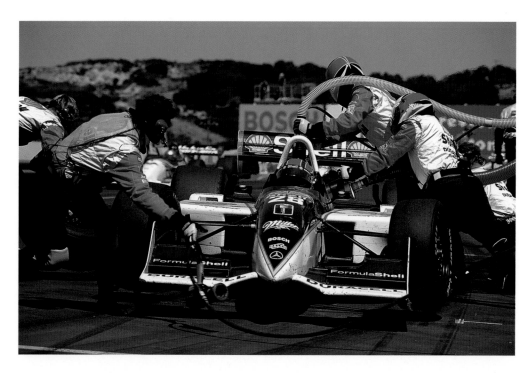

New teammate Bryan Herta picked up his pace in the season's second half. Here Bryan makes a pit stop at Laguna Seca, where he qualified and finished second after a furious battle with Alex Zanardi. (Paul Webb)

In 1996, CART held its own Memorial Day event at Michigan instead of racing at Indianapolis. At the start, there was a massive accident when Adrian Fernandez plowed into Jimmy Vasser and Herta, and they all hit the wall. "It was so unrepresentative of the quality of the drivers," Bobby remembers, "But after all this talk about how great we were, it was almost as if it were preordained." (Michael C. Brown)

obviously had a bad situation with Ganassi, and I thought with our team he could grow and realize his potential."

In his first year with Team Rahal, Herta finished eighth in the championship, directly behind his new boss and team leader. Bryan was second in the midsummer Marlboro 500 at Michigan and led half the race at Laguna Seca at season's end, only to be passed by Alex Zanardi in a now famous move: under braking at the Corkscrew on the last lap. Bobby beat Bryan in the championship by one place and sixteen points. Bobby's best races came in Toronto, where he was third, and near season's end, at Elkhart Lake and Vancouver, where he took a pair of seconds, both times hard on the tail of winner Michael Andretti.

The Indianapolis 500 was missing from Bobby's agenda in 1996 for the first time in fifteen years. Fueled with talk of cutting costs, encouraging more American short-track drivers, and committing to racing strictly on ovals, Indianapolis Motor Speedway president

Tony George turned his back on CART in 1996 and created his own Indy Racing League series. During the painful time of the separation, Bobby was a vocal proponent of CART's cause versus the concept of the IRL and was as heartbroken as anyone at the failure to find common ground with Tony George.

"It's still a huge distraction and frustration," Bobby admits. "It's a negative for open-wheel racing, no matter how people want to paint it. I think it should be clear to all parties that there has to be some kind of a compromise. As long as you overturn every stone to try to find a solution, then you can sleep at night and present your case to your sponsors and the people who follow the sport, and let the chips fall where they may. But until there's absolutely no hope, I don't think you can give up."

For years, Indy car racing's "old guard" had argued vehemently with CART about restricting the ever escalating costs and technology. The most prominent among them were the Indianapolis 500's sanctioning body, the United States Automobile Club (USAC); driver and team owner A. J. Foyt; and, eventually, George, whose family also owns the track. USAC's inability to deal effectively with these cost and technology issues in the seventies was a key factor in the creation of CART as a sanctioning body in 1979.

CART believed in restricting but not banning new technology. It felt the cost of racing would be offset by increasing the size of the audience and attracting greater sponsorship. USAC and George had long been convinced that moving to less expensive stock-block engines was part of the solution, but CART did not want to accept the performance limitations that move would entail. George was also opposed to the increasing number of races held on road courses and street circuits, and believed Indy cars should race exclusively on oval tracks.

CART's board of directors is made up exclusively of team owners, but in an effort to accommodate him, they invited George to serve on the board on an experimental basis in 1993 and 1994. He eventually decided not to continue with CART, and the team owners agreed that their views were incompatible, citing not only differences in philosophy but also USAC's continuing to make what the board considered to be shortsighted rule changes, as in the case of the 209-cubic-inch pushrod engine, when the boost limit was changed twice in the months following the 1994 Indianapolis 500.

Near the end of 1998, George extended his commitment to the IRL's more restrictive formula through 2004, further delaying hopes that CART's drivers and teams will ever again race at Indianapolis. Like every driver who raced there, let alone those few who actually won the Indy 500 when it genuinely was the "World's Greatest Race," Bobby looks back warmly on the fourteen months of May he spent there.

During 1995 and 1996 a political battle was waged between CART and the IRL's Tony George. Bobby was one of the most eloquent and vocal proponents of CART during this unhappy time. (Paul Webb)

At Mid-Ohio, Bobby is joined by Graham on the victory podium. Bobby finished third behind Alex Zanardi and Greg Moore. Zanardi won the first of his two PPG Cup titles that year, while Moore became the youngest winner in Champ car history. (Dan Boyd)

"There are three things I miss about the month of May. I miss driving over there from Columbus with my belongings and my clothes in the back of my car. You know you are about to embark on a month, and there's the anticipation and the hope, you name it. Every day when you drove into that track, you said to yourself 'OK, what have you got in store for me today?' "

"I miss qualifying—the most pressure-packed four laps I think in any race-car driver's life who's ever done Indy. If you just blipped the throttle a little bit and lost two-tenths of a mile an hour it could mean the difference between one row or making the field. No matter how prepared you were on Friday night, it could all go south on Saturday morning. And then race day, of course. Race day was really something very special.

"But everything else I hated. It was such a fierce environment of pressure, day in, day out. Driving in every day and looking for that tenth of a mile an hour. And of course, everything in the whole town was focused on what's happening at the speedway. Every TV and radio station, every newspaper, was filled with it."

Bobby views the philosophical differences between CART and the IRL in this way: "I don't disagree with the IRL's chassis rules in terms of freezing certain aspects of the costs, because we do need to make our series financially more responsible. Having said that, it won't make it cheaper, because if you look at NASCAR, which is a highly restrictive formula, you'd say it can't be very expensive. Yet that series is more expensive than CART. The top NASCAR teams are spending more money each year than we do, as much as $10 million and more for a one-car team, because the more restrictions there are, the more money is devoted to finding the loopholes, or the little intricacies, that make the difference."

Bobby is pragmatic about the financial realities of motor racing. "It's a misrepresentation to promote that racing has never been expensive. It's always been whoever has the most money won. That's the reality. Racing wraps itself in the belief that it's the sport of the little guy, but it has never been the sport of the little guy. The little guys make up the numbers, but the guys that win are the ones with the resources.

"I don't care if you're talking about Indianapolis in 1950, or '90, or Formula One. You name it. Whoever has the technology, or the money, or the genius, it's those advantages that make the difference. This type of racing is probably now as democratic as it's ever been in terms of the level of competition and the different number of winners."

In every major form of racing, there is no question that a strong alliance with a motor manufacturer is essential to success and will be even more important in the future. Toward that end, Bobby changed engine suppliers again for 1997, switching to Ford-Cosworth.

Rain added to the challenge of the Road America round. Bobby moved up from eleventh on the grid at Elkhart in 1997 to finish sixth. (Jon Eisberg)

Bobby hoped the move would create technical synergy between Team Rahal and Ford and be a relationship that would last for many years.

"Dan Rivard and I had a pretty good relationship," Bobby comments. "I guess I probably sat down with him some time and just said, 'You know, I would have gone with you guys for 1995 had we known you had a pushrod on the drawing board.'

"One of the biggest reasons in my decision to go with Ford, aside from Dan, was my desire for a strategic partnership where, if we did our job and we made things available for Ford, there would be a trading of technology and people where the sum was greater than the parts. We look at Team Rahal as an ideal place for Ford to teach young engineers, to give them experience, and conversely, we think they bring a value to us.

"That means having assistance with developing the chassis and aerodynamics, the whole technological package. We were willing to share proprietary technical information that I think a lot of other teams weren't. We basically opened the books up. We put total trust in Ford Motor Company, and that trust hasn't been violated in any respect. We really said, 'Here's the key to the door. Have at it.' I felt the risk was far less than the reward for us. By being open and honest with them, we can develop a relationship that both of us want to develop, and it's working that way."

"I knew I couldn't get that with Mercedes because of Roger [Penske]. It's Roger's baby. I couldn't get it with Honda because that bridge had been burned, I guess. Ford and I had talked about dating for so many years, and finally we actually decided to *go* on a date. The courtship was a long one. I mean, I was the last guy to win a race with the original Cosworth DFX in 1989, until the XB won in 1992 with Michael."

It turned out that 1997 was not a good year as a whole, although both Bobby and Bryan had their moments. Bobby qualified third in Brazil and drove a superb race, leading 102 of 133 laps until he ran out of fuel going into the last lap. He again made the podium at Mid-Ohio with a great drive from sixteenth to third, and in Vancouver he qualified second and took the lead after Zanardi crashed, only to suffer a blown engine early in the race. Bryan showed his stuff by taking the pole at Mid-Ohio and Laguna Seca, and he led both races until his tires failed him. His best result was third at Cleveland as Team Rahal finished a disappointing eleventh and twelfth in points, Bryan ahead of Bobby.

At the U.S. 500 in July on the superfast, high-banked Michigan Speedway, Bobby emerged bruised but unhurt from a huge 65g accident. He qualified sixth at Michigan and ran up front in the race, leading twenty-five laps in the middle of the 500 miles until crashing heavily in the second turn. While lapping Dennis Vitolo, Bobby got too high in the first turn, drifted into the tire "marbles," and smacked hard into the wall. The wreckage slid partway down the backstretch before coming to a stop. Bobby emphasizes that once the accident began, there was no time to even think about recovering or correcting.

CART's medical director, Dr. Steve Olvey, says the most important factor in crash safety is the rate of speed reduction on impact rather than the speed itself. Bobby was a testament to the theory that day as he emerged uninjured from the wreckage. After a physical check, he was able to make his planned flight to Scotland that evening and was on the links the following day enjoying a five-day golfing vacation.

Bobby is reasonably satisfied with where things stand with CART's well-proven cars. Frustrating as the struggle is to reduce or control performance, great strides have been made since the early '80s in crash safety.

"There's not a lot more we can do," Bobby says. "I don't think you're going to see huge jumps in safety performance. I think our minimum weight is adequate. We don't need to be

Right: Herta, starting from pole, leads the field away at Laguna Seca. He led the first twenty-one laps before his tires lost all grip and he faded to finish sixth. A similar experience for Herta at Mid-Ohio a month earlier played a large role in Bobby's decision to switch from Goodyear to Firestone for 1998. (Paul Webb)

MICHIGAN SPEEDWAY

lighter, because the lighter we go, the more esoteric materials we need to have, and the more costs go up, and ultimately, I think, the less safe the driver is. What we have right now are very safe and stable cars. We've seen other organizations produce slower cars that are compromised as far as safety, and that's the last thing we want to do.

"Irrespective of how fast the cars are going," Bobby adds, "you will always drive the car on the edge. You will always trim it out and try to run as little downforce as you can to try to maximize the performance of the car. It's ludicrous to think that if you reduce speeds by 10 or 20 MPH there won't be any more accidents. People will start to run the car more and more on the edge looking for more performance."

He also emphasizes the deep respect any Champ car driver has for a superspeedway. "A racing driver has a tremendous conflict in himself that he wants to go fast but wants to be safe," Bobby notes. "One thing about any oval track like Michigan or California is leaving the place. Walking out and driving home is always a special feeling because you know any accident you're going to have there is going to be a big one. And yet when you leave those places, if you've won or done well, you're ten feet high. You feel like you've really done something."

"We've proven we can still pedal the car."

For much of 1997, Bobby found himself thinking more and more about retiring from driving. After the season was over, he scheduled a press conference at Team Rahal headquarters in November to announce that 1998 would be his final year as a driver. He made the announcement with Miller Brewing's sports marketing director, Mike Welsh, and CART CEO, Andrew Craig. Bobby and Mike revealed that Bobby's final year would be called "Rahal's Last Ride," with a charitable fund-raising campaign tied in.

"I've thought about this decision for many, many months," Bobby said at the "Last Ride" announcement. "There has been a lot of consideration toward my family, because of the demands that this sport puts on an individual as a driver, let alone as an owner-driver, and in terms of what the needs of the company are in the future. Twenty-five years ago when I began racing, I never anticipated being in the position that I am today. I started racing purely because I loved it, and I enjoyed the people that were connected with it. Fortunately, I can say those things still remain quite strong.

Above: Nestled deep in the cockpit of his Reynard-Ford, Bobby enjoyed his final experiences of life at 200-plus MPH. It's something he recalls fondly but insists he doesn't miss. (Jon Eisberg)

Opposite: Bobby waves to the crowd at the midsummer U.S. 500 at Michigan. To reduce speeds, CART had all cars run with the "Handford Wing," essentially a five-inch-deep blade that closed off the back of the rear wing like a box-flap. It added drag and decreased downforce. It also made the competition intense. Bobby, who finished seventh, was only 2.39 seconds behind winner Greg Moore. (Michael C. Brown)

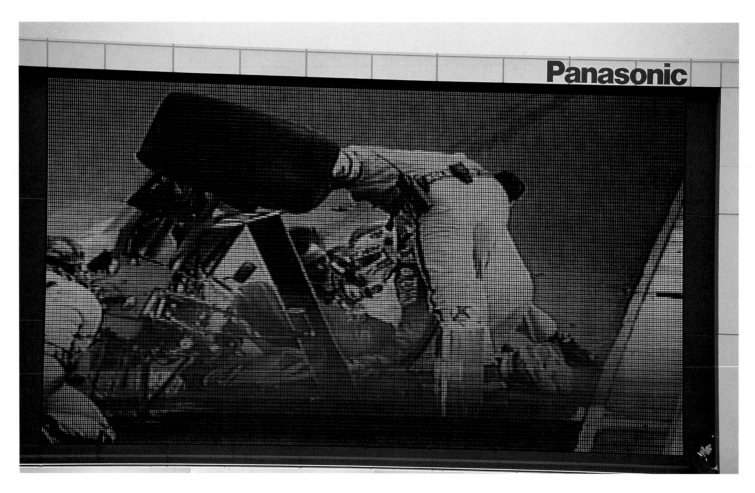

A giant TV screen on the back stretch at Japan's Twin-Ring Motegi oval shows Bobby scrambling out of his overturned car after a wheel bearing failed late in the race. He had charged from near the back of the field to third place and was closing rapidly on leaders Adrian Fernandez and Al Unser Jr. when the accident occurred. (Paul Webb)

"In those twenty-five years, I've achieved far more than I ever dreamt or thought possible. So it's not with a heavy heart, but with a lot of happiness and sense of satisfaction, that I can make an announcement of this nature."

Bobby thanked his family; the car owners, sponsors, and mechanics who had been instrumental to his career; and particularly Debi for her support as a wife, mother, and driving force behind the man. "She's seen the good and the bad, the disappointments and the victories. She's been my little-league mother," he said. "She's the one that's out there pushing all the time. I think she's more aggressive than I am in many respects."

During the off-season Bobby underwent laser eye surgery, which eliminated his need to wear glasses. The surgery was performed in Columbus by Dr. Curt Kelley. "It was really a quality-of-life issue," Bobby says. "I could never wear contacts because of the astigmatism I had. The contacts had to be weighted, and every time I would blink, everything would go fuzzy for a second before it cleared up."

Another important change for Bobby's final season was a switch from longtime tire supplier Goodyear to Firestone. Starting with its re-entry into Indy and Champ car racing in 1995 after a twenty-year absence, Firestone began to thrash Goodyear, winning more races each year, including the last eighteen in a row of 1998's nineteen races. In 1997, Herta had lost chances to win at Mid-Ohio and Laguna Seca when his Goodyears literally fell apart. The decision to switch was obvious for Team Rahal.

Despite his enthusiasm for a competitive final year, Bobby was conspicuously noncompetitive in the 1998 season opener on the 1.5-mile Homestead oval in Florida. He qualified seventeenth and finished nineteenth, three laps down, after struggling all the way with an evil-handling car. After the race, he had some stern words with his engineers and Tim Cindric. "I was really upset, because we just completely missed on the setup that weekend," Bobby says, shaking his head. "It couldn't have been a worse way to start the year."

The unvarnished conversation had a positive effect. Two weeks later at the sparkling new Twin-Ring Motegi oval built by Honda in the mountains north of Tokyo, Bobby ran very well. He started seventeenth because qualifying was rained out and the lineup was determined by practice times, but he knew he had a good car and demonstrated it in spades on race day.

Bobby charged through the field to third place in the final stages and was closing in on leaders Adrian Fernandez and Al Unser Jr. But with just sixteen laps to go, a wheel bearing failed, and he crashed spectacularly. His car clouted the wall, flipped onto its side, and slithered across the track to a stop. It was a scary-looking accident, but with the assistance of CART's safety team, Bobby wriggled out of the wreckage, a little shaken, but without a scratch.

At Long Beach the next weekend, Bobby qualified and ran second to impressive teammate Herta before losing two laps in an infuriating, multicar incident that was none of his

On lap 19 Bobby's race at Surfers Paradise came to an unhappy end when he hit the wall. He had started eleventh and had been pushing hard to move up through the field. (Dan Boyd)

Bryan and Bobby shared the front row at Long Beach. Herta led a
quarter of the race, but was beaten in the end by Alex Zanardi,
while Bobby ran equally well and turned the race's fastest lap, only
to lose five laps in a multicar incident. (Paul Webb)

doing. After sitting there stalled, frustrated, and waving for help, he came back to set the race's fastest lap only five laps from the finish, further proof that the fire still burned fiercely in his heart. He finished in the top six at Nazareth, Milwaukee, and Portland and enjoyed another strong street race in July in Toronto, where he finished fourth, within 2 seconds of third-place Jimmy Vasser.

In August, Bobby came from sixteenth to finish third at Mid-Ohio, just 2.4 seconds behind winner Adrian Fernandez in his best finish of his final season. "I wanted to make my last twenty laps at Mid-Ohio the best I've ever driven here," Bobby said after the race. "Every lap was like qualifying, and I think I set my fastest lap with three laps to go. Most importantly for me, when my fellow drivers kid me about their being fast, I can sit there and look at them and say, 'Hey kid, you're half my age and I'm faster than you are!' I think we've proven we still can pedal the car. I'm not going through the motions."

The year was filled with celebratory functions and appearances, and Bobby readily admitted at Mid-Ohio that it already had been a very tiring season. At every race, however, and not least Mid-Ohio, his heart was warmed by the enthusiasm of the fans and by signs declaring, "Thank You Bobby," or "We'll Miss You," or "Thanks for the Memories."

"It's been very fatiguing," Bobby said at Mid-Ohio, "although I must say I look forward to Thursday night of each race weekend because usually all the functions are over by that point. But on Sunday morning, when we go 'round the track in the drivers' parades and see all the signs and hear the cheers from the fans, well, it's been more than I've ever hoped for, frankly. It makes you feel like you actually did something worthwhile over the last twenty-five years.

"As much as I looked forward to this week," he added, "I faced it with a little bit of trepidation because there was so much going on. Everybody was wishing me well and if you let it, you can forget you're here for a race. When we came in this morning, and I saw the banners saying, 'Thanks for the memories,' my wife and my kids were crying. I was emotional, too."

Bobby leads Bryan at Nazareth, where they finished sixth and eighth, respectively. An indication of the fierce competition in Champ car racing during Bobby's retirement season was that he crossed the line only 9 seconds behind winner Jimmy Vasser. (Paul Webb)

"I think the year has been a success," Bobby quietly mulled a few days after the race at Mid-Ohio. "We've been in the hunt. We've qualified very well. I want to win one last race. We've got that to do, but I have no doubts that I can compete on speed."

The following weekend, he qualified on the inside of the second row at Road America and was right in the hunt in the race, but the team messed up badly on pit-stop strategy. After two more stops than everyone else, he finished half a lap behind in eighth place. As he had after the year's first race, Bobby again had angry words with Tim Cindric and his engineers.

Before the next race in Vancouver, Bobby flew to Miller Brewing's headquarters in Milwaukee to announce that twenty-five-year-old Italian, Max Papis, would take his place in 1999. All spring and summer Bobby had been looking for the right man to step into his shoes, and to the surprise of many, the relatively unheralded Papis got the job. Papis broke into Champ car racing in 1996 with Arciero-Wells's Toyota-powered team, replacing Jeff

Above: The Rahal family acknowledges the applause from Bobby's hometown fans on the drivers' parade lap before his last race at Mid-Ohio. This was a very emotional day for Bobby, Debi, and their children. (Michael C. Brown)

Opposite: With so many of his fans urging him on, Bobby wanted his last race at Mid-Ohio to be something special. Responding like the champion he is, Bobby put in a great performance and drove his way up to third place at the checkered flag, only 2.4 seconds behind winner Adrian Fernandez. (Michael C. Brown)

Krosnoff, who was killed at Toronto in July of that year. Toyota's engines couldn't match the power of CART's big three—Honda, Ford, and Mercedes-Benz—but Papis put in many spirited performances and produced Toyota's best results in 1997 and 1998.

"I didn't even know Max was available until he came up to me in the hotel at Michigan in July," Bobby explains. "I think he was frustrated because he had done all the groundwork for the Toyota project after he replaced Jeff Krosnoff, and yet Robby [Gordon] was getting the good engines. He felt like all the effort he put forward had kind of been for naught. So I said I'd think about it, and I talked to my guys."

"I just see in Max a young man with great hunger and desire. He's got great charisma. I think Max is the kind of guy who can energize a team. He's renowned for his work with sponsors, but for us the most important thing was we needed to make sure we had a guy who could run up front and win. It's been difficult to compare Max to anybody because of what he had to deal with, but when you compare him against Robby, I thought he compared very well. And I think we've made a great choice. We talked to Jimmy [Vasser]. We talked to Richie [Hearn]. We talked to a number of people, but when it was understood that Max was available, we didn't waste any time.

"Bryan and Max are very different people. Bryan's very determined but quiet. With Max, everything's right there on his sleeve. And I think a team needs both those kind of people."

A few weeks later, at Laguna Seca, Herta came through both for himself and the team as he scored his first victory in his seventieth Champ car start and the team's first in ninety-eight races, since Bobby had won at Nazareth in 1992. Herta was on the pole and led all the way, save for pit stops, fending off a late challenge from double CART champion Alex Zanardi, who had beaten Bryan at this track two years before with a famous last-lap pass at the Corkscrew.

"I think we've been very patient with Bryan," Bobby reflected a few weeks later, "and frankly, as I told the people in our team, Bryan was right on the cusp of moving from being the most likely to succeed to becoming the *least* likely to succeed. You can only be most likely to succeed for so long, and at some point, you're just not going to get it done."

Bobby said there were races he felt Bryan should have won in 1998, although he defended his driver for the first-turn accident at Mid-Ohio. "At Long Beach, he had an opportunity to win that race, and maybe he didn't fight hard enough to try to keep Zanardi at bay. At Nazareth, he led a lot of the race and literally in the space of a few laps went a lap

down. There was some concern on our part, but I will say I think he was unfairly branded at Mid-Ohio [where Herta and pole man Dario Franchitti collided at the apex, taking Jimmy Vasser with them]. I think that was his corner. I think that was a case where, yes, maybe Bryan was too aggressive coming in, but I think Dario could have let off, and they both would've made it around to fight later."

Bobby freely admits the team lost Portland for Herta in 1998. "We basically screwed him. The strategy in the pits was the wrong one. He was leading the race, and after the stops he ended up third, but I think his win at Laguna was monumental in its meaning to him and to everybody. He beat the right guy at the right place at the right time.

"Now Bryan's got to prove that he can do it again. But he answered a lot of critics with that win at Laguna and justified, to a large extent, the belief that we had in him."

Bobby said at the time that Herta's Laguna win was the team's greatest victory. "We'd been so close so many times—me in Brazil in 1997 and Bryan at various places—that pretty soon you begin to wonder what you have to do to win one of these things. You look around and see other teams and, without offense, we feel we're a better team, and yet they're winning and we're not. What are they doing, and what are we not doing? For us, that win was getting the monkey not just off his back, but getting the collective monkey off our backs as well."

After the morning warmup before Bobby's last race, the Marlboro 500 at the California Speedway in Fontana, Bobby drives down pit road to the applause of all the teams, whose crews donned Bobby look-alike Groucho Marx-type horn-rimmed glasses, noses, and mustaches. (Paul Webb)

Bobby knew all along that the season-ending Marlboro 500 at the California Speedway would be a particularly difficult weekend, not only because it was his last race but also because of the intimidating, potentially lethal nature of the high-banked 2-mile superspeedway. He also had a thick guest list that weekend, including, among many others, his mom and dad, Letterman, and Wiley McCoy.

"From a personal standpoint, it's going to be a very tough race because there will be so many people there that were so important to me over the years," he said a few weeks before the race. "My parents, my wife and my kids, and many people who helped make my career happen will all be there. I've been thinking about it during the year. What's it going to be like on Saturday night when I get into bed? Am I going to sit there and think about everything? What am I going to do?"

Things went well in practice and qualifying. Bobby qualified fifth, his best for a 500-mile race since 1992, his last championship year. At the drivers' meeting on Saturday afternoon he was presented with the last of a series of gifts from longtime rival and friend Al Unser Jr., who performed the task on behalf of the drivers as president of the Championship Drivers Association.

"At each race through the season, Al made all the drivers listen to all my results at that track," Bobby recalls with a smile. "Some races I didn't mind because we'd only been there once a year, but some tracks, like Michigan, I'd been there seventeen years, and we had two races a year for some of those years, so there were twenty or twenty-one results. Al enjoyed poking a little fun at me with these long-winded lists."

On Sunday, at the end of the traditional half-hour morning warmup session, Bobby was asked to do an extra lap and cruise slowly down the pit lane to receive the applause of all the teams. To his great amusement, everyone in the pit lane saluted him by donning identical, Groucho Marx–like horn-rimmed glasses with attached noses and mustaches, mimicking Bobby's mid-'80s appearance.

A few hours later, after the usual demanding combination of the prerace technical and strategic debriefing followed by speeches at lunch to sponsors and team guests, it was down to business for the last start of his career. For a while things looked good as Bobby settled into position with the leaders, running right there in fifth or sixth, feeling comfortable and capable of challenging at any time. But then his car's handling began to deteriorate, getting more and more tail-happy, or loose, the worst possible feeling to have on a 230 MPH superspeedway.

The team hoped to find an advantage by choosing a different sequence of pit stops, but it didn't materialize, and Bobby fell a lap behind. On a restart with just five laps to go, teammate Herta and Bobby's replacement, Max Papis, tangled directly in front of Bobby. Herta and Papis ended their races in the wall as Bobby threaded his way through the wreckage without incident. "I hope that's not the future of Team Rahal," Bobby half-joked after the race.

A delighted Herta pops the bubbly after his long-awaited victory. It took seventy races for Bryan to score his breakthrough win. It also marked the team's first win in ninety-eight races, since Nazareth in 1992. (Dan Boyd)

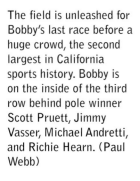

The mess from the Herta-Papis accident was rapidly cleaned up, but there was only time enough for a one-lap sprint to the checkered flag, wherein Ganassi teammates, Jimmy Vasser and Alex Zanardi, got the jump on Greg Moore so that Vasser was narrowly able to defeat Moore with Zanardi third. Bobby came home eleventh, one lap down, running as quickly as the leaders near the end, and crossed the line just a quarter of a second behind twenty-three-year old Brazilian rookie, Helio Castro-Neves.

"We were still trying," Bobby said. "Somebody said, what did I feel on the last lap? And I said I was pissed because I didn't pass Castro-Neves. I was still trying right till the end."

Bobby finished his final season tenth in points, beating Al Jr., among others, so that 1997 was the only one of his seventeen years in CART that Bobby finished out of the top ten. "More than anything, I think I retired on a competitive note, and that was my objective. I can look back on this year and point to a number of races where we figured in the race, and that's what I'm pleased about. I'm very pleased to be in the top ten, even if it's tenth."

In his last post-race interview as a driver, Bobby described his immediate feelings and reflections. "I don't feel melancholy or sadness or joy, necessarily, or any of those emotions you might think I would feel. I just know that a long chapter in my life is over and now a new chapter has started. Where that chapter will take me, I have no idea, but I hope it's about winning races in the future and to be a positive influence on open-wheel racing in this country. Really, the most obvious thing I feel is the fact that there's a new day, starting now."

The field is unleashed for Bobby's last race before a huge crowd, the second largest in California sports history. Bobby is on the inside of the third row behind pole winner Scott Pruett, Jimmy Vasser, Michael Andretti, and Richie Hearn. (Paul Webb)

Bobby shakes longtime crew chief Jimmy Prescott's hand as he climbs out of a race car for the last time, ending a career that spanned twenty-nine years and more than 450 races, including 264 Champ car races. (Paul Webb)

Index